Praising Girls Well

**Other books available from Da Capo Press
by Elizabeth Hartley-Brewer**

Praising Boys Well

Talking to Tweens

Raising a Self-Starter

Raising Confident Boys

Raising Confident Girls

Raising Happy Kids

Praising Girls Well

100 Tips for Parents and Teachers

ELIZABETH HARTLEY-BREWER

Da Capo

LIFE LONG

A Member of the
Perseus Books Group

For Julia, with admiration and appreciation

————————

Set in 10-point Stone Serif by the Perseus Books Group

Library of Congress Cataloging-in-Publication Data

Hartley-Brewer, Elizabeth.
    Praising girls well : 100 tips for parents and teachers / Elizabeth
Hartley-Brewer. — 1st ed.
        p.   cm.
    ISBN-13: 978-0-7382-1022-3 (pbk. : alk. paper)
    ISBN-10: 0-7382-1022-6 (pbk. : alk. paper) 1. Girls. 2. Praise.
3. Child rearing. 4. Self-esteem in children. 5. Parent and child.
6. Teacher-student relationships. I. Title.
HQ777.H289 2006
649'.133—dc22   2005028286

First Da Capo Press edition 2006

Published by Da Capo Press
A Member of the Perseus Books Group
http://www.dacapopress.com

Da Capo Press books are available at special discounts for
bulk purchases in the U.S. by corporations, institutions,
and other organizations. For more information, please contact the
Special Markets Department at the Perseus Books Group,
11 Cambridge Center, Cambridge, MA 02142, or call
(800) 255-1514 or (617) 252-5298, or
e-mail special.markets@perseusbooks.com.

1 2 3 4 5 6 7 8 9—09 08 07 06

Contents

Introduction

T his book is for parents with girls of any age—babies, toddlers and teenagers—and for teachers. Most of the tips cover general principles, but several are age-specific and show how our praise style should change as our daughters grow. One of the most important lessons we have learned over the last two to three decades is how much all children benefit from receiving praise from parents and teachers. Children respond far better to positive feedback and encouragement than they do to threats, criticism, and punishment. Many parents and teachers once found what they felt to be flattering words hard to use, and although some still find it hard, most people are now sufficiently familiar and comfortable with the phrases most commonly used to hand out praise in good measure.

Praise has been viewed as the way to boost children's self-esteem, to help them feel confident, and to help them fulfill their potential and be at ease with themselves. Many won't realize that using praise also has wider benefits for individual children and for society: It can help to encourage self-discipline and moral behavior. However, nothing about parenting or children is straightforward. Boys and girls, for example, often react to praise in different ways and need their confidence reinforced in different areas. We are also beginning to realize that if praise is overused, used for particular personal motives, or directed at the wrong kind of activity, it may actually be unhelpful. When praise is overused, overhyped or belies the truth, a girl may either become praise-dependent and require constant affirmation and approval or become indifferent to it. Another possibility is that she may start to mistrust either the message or the messenger, wasting everyone's breath; or she might come to think she's superclever and special and annoy people with her self-importance, when in truth she's simply normal. Any child can also feel suffocated by a continuous positive or negative commentary on her every move, and she may act out to shake off the microscopic attention and constant judgment.

In addition, there is growing concern that overexposure to praise has led to children being ruined by rewards, dulled by "dumbing down," and incapacitated by anxiety or, at the very least, easily wrong-footed when faced with real challenges. They may then conceal their anxiety with diversionary displays of daring and risk taking in other spheres. For praise to be reliably effective, we have to be careful and subtle and understand fully its pros and cons, wider value, and the approaches that are safest given girls' particular sensitivities.

This is what this book sets out to achieve. The early chapters (1–6) present the basic principles, tactics, and purposes of praise. Chapter 1 develops an understanding of praise that underpins the thinking behind the 100 tips, which are spread equally among the remaining ten chapters. Chapter 4 enables readers to reflect upon important features of child development and so relate the principles and tactics to the age and developmental stage of any girl. The later chapters (7–10) consider the subtleties and potential dangers of praise, and Chapter 11, the final chapter, invites readers to self-reflect. Each tip has been written to stand alone and so the lists can be dipped into at random, but readers may benefit initially from reading consecutively at least the introduction to each chapter to gain a sense of the direction and argument. It is a book to revisit on many occasions.

To show what this book will cover, look at the following questions and consider why the difference between the possible responses might be important.

When your daughter does particularly well, which might you say?

- I'm really proud of you for managing that!
- I hope you feel proud of yourself—you should.
- You probably feel really proud to have achieved that.
- I feel so proud of you and proud that you're my child.

If your daughter makes the school swimming team, would you . . . ?

- Say, "Great! How many others tried for how many places?"
- Promise to continue the trips to the pool to develop her skills further.
- Go as a family to every swim meet to give her support.
- Attend the meets yourself and shout encouragement from the side.

When your daughter tidies her room without being told, would you . . . ?

- Give her a hug and bring her a treat to eat.
- Say thanks, but laugh and say you wonder how long it will last.
- Give her money, and hope this will persuade her to carry on the good work.
- Comment favorably on the improvement and ask what triggered the idea.

As you will discover in this book, praising well is a subtle art, and the way in which you phrase it can make a huge difference in whether a child feels freed and encouraged by your comments or, despite your good intentions, becomes anxious because she senses a pressure to do even better. As you read through the 100 tips that follow, you will come to appreciate the benefit of beginning most of your comments with *you* rather than *I*, of encouraging your daughter to judge her own efforts rather than rely on your view, of not taking any credit for the success, and of focusing on her reasons for and feelings about doing well, not yours.

Now read on!

Praising Girls Well

Chapter 1

Understanding Praise and How Girls React to It

Children love praise; of course they do, for most of us thrive on compliments and appreciation. Despite the pleasure it gives, children should be praised for more than just the delight it brings them or the help it gives them to try harder. Praise needs to be a central part of raising children because it meets most of their fundamental needs. In other words, praise is not merely a bit of luxury, some additional fancy wrapping that we can leave out if we prefer. Children need to feel important and significant to someone, to believe that someone cares enough to cherish them, and this is at least as important as being properly fed and clothed. Children need to feel secure and to trust and rely on that care, which they can when they feel valued and central to their carer's life. They also need friendly and warm guidance, support, and direction about how they should lead their lives through to adolescence, so they need to hear what it is they should do rather than how they constantly fall short and disappoint. And in order for children to flourish, they need to know and be told they are capable, are enjoyed, and give pleasure—particularly to their parents.

Praise tends to be thought of as something spoken, put into words, but we can convey our pleasure, approval, and appreciation in many ways. Hugs, smiles, rewards, and touches, as we see in Chapter 6, all have their part to play and can sometimes be more effective because they can be more spontaneous and more direct. Even the spoken vocabulary of praise is more varied than at first appears, for the term *praise* includes many types of phrase and expression that convey approval, appreciation, acknowledgment, and pure delight. The differences are important, as will become clear as the tips are explored.

It is deeply frustrating to realize that not all praise is helpful: Just when we thought we were getting it right, people are saying we could be getting it wrong. The good news is that it is not complicated to work out which styles and phrases are likely to support achievement and which sentiments can become confusing or burdensome and could cause our children difficulty. Effective relationships are always those that manage to keep a range of needs, styles, and objectives in balance. The essence of constructive praise is that it is useful and encouraging: It provides relevant, detailed information; it is believable so it is neither hollow nor false; and it may also show the way forward. Most important, the recipient should remain in full charge of her progress and be given opportunities to become confident in her ability to judge things for herself.

The energy that enables girls to take advantage of opportunity is self-belief. Self-belief is fueled when girls feel genuinely capable because they know in detail what it was they did right (which means they know they can do it again), because they have acknowledged the mistakes they've made in the past and now know how to avoid them (which means failures have been faced, not ignored), and because they feel certain that they are unconditionally loved and accepted for who they are, not for matching up to someone else's ideal or for something they're especially good at. It is rarely helpful to celebrate every success and ignore every failure, for just as certain types of praise can be unhelpful, criticism can be constructive—when mistakes are acknowledged, identified, and ironed out, girls learn from them.

Girls tend to be more conformist than boys and like to toe the line and receive approval. Most enjoy being "good," to the extent that girls are the goody-goodies and are far more likely to strive to be teacher's pet. Few boys are ever described as a goody-goody. But the danger is that girls have a propensity to do something not because they judge it to be right or helpful but in order to get into or stay in other people's good graces. They are therefore far more prey to flattery than boys, more likely to mold themselves on key individuals' expectations, and can become cut off from their true selves, which means that they may have fewer opportunities to establish a clear personal identity.

With girls, it is important not to overemphasize "good" behavior. Obedience, diligence, cleanliness, and tidiness are certainly easier for parents to live with, but far more than this is required if a child is to become a successful adult. Eating-disorder specialists comment frequently on female sufferers' perfectionism, their regular handwriting, their impressive personal organization, and their sensitivity, high standards and achievements, and desire to please. Yet this success often masks a deep discontent and doubt directed at the self. What girls need in today's competitive world is the ability to stand up for themselves, to explore, be creative, and take risks, which raises the likelihood of mistakes and mess. Praise needs to boost a girl's inner confidence—her underlying capacities and her ability to trust her own judgment—rather than to highlight effort and outcomes that have been defined as desirable by someone else. When girls become "clones" and model themselves on an idealized image to get approval, it can mean that they fear failure.

Girls enjoy pleasing adults and respect success in others, so they remain happy to receive praise publicly. Their achievements may encourage others to greater effort, but some may become bitchy to offset the envy they feel. Despite clear success, those who do well often remain sure it was a fluke, not due to their talent. They need to be given detail about what they did right to convince them, and they should be told that it is absolutely okay to make mistakes and fail sometimes.

Chapter 2

The Purpose of Praise

What is praise for? It may seem an unnecessary question to ask but it is important to be clear about what it is we are trying to achieve to help us check whether what we say and do is all-around beneficial with no negative side effects. For example, parents, of course, want to help their daughter grow up with good self-esteem to confound the age-old assumption that women do not or cannot make it to the top: Self-esteem and strong self-belief are, indeed, valuable attributes. Nonetheless, their value is undermined if they come at the expense of sound self-knowledge (because she is told she's wonderful at everything), of sound friendships (because friends are put off by her resulting busybody bossiness), and of determination and perseverance (because she is always shielded from challenges and setbacks). Praising certain reactions and behavior can encourage the development of moral awareness by encouraging children to notice other people's helpful behavior and commenting favorably on thoughtfulness, but if piling on praise leads to self-obsession and overconfidence, a girl's awareness of her impact on other people could be dulled. In order to decide whether our affirmative comments and actions are overall helpful, we should acknowledge the full range of possible desirable goals and the different categories and styles of positive feedback.

Here are some terms that help us to focus on the varied, deeper purposes of praise beyond the obvious ones: *affirm; appreciate; approve; admire; attend; anticipate; achieve; acknowledge; be aware and alert; aspiration.*

Each of these ten simple objectives is explored as a separate tip in this chapter.

It is useful to consider praise in terms of time zones. Although each encounter and incident is in the present, a key purpose of praise—and of support and encouragement—is to help our daughters or the girls in our charge feel optimistic about their future, comfortable with the route they have traveled from the past, and content with the present. When we *encourage* them, our focus is on the future—we try to convince any girl she will overcome any current difficulty to be successful hereafter. We therefore generate faith, hope, and confidence and give her heart. When we clearly *enjoy* her company and achievements, we indicate our happiness and pleasure with who she is, in the present. When we *endorse* her actions, her view of the world, her approaches to learning, and her feelings, we are accepting those bits of her that have been fashioned by her past. If girls are comfortable about their past behavior and experiences, even if these were difficult, they are better able to look optimistically at the future. It is not helpful for parents or significant others to make a girl either ashamed of or guilty about her past or to dismiss it in any attempt to refocus and start again.

> Q: *If parents don't praise you directly, how else might you know that they're pleased with you?*
>
> A: *You can tell by their face, which shows they're proud.*
>
> —Alice, age 8
>
> A: *They might be nice to me in the evening and let me do more things.*
>
> —Jenni, age 15

To affirm a child is to make a clear statement that confirms and accepts her as she is. The word has its origins in a Latin word that means "strong." It therefore implies strength. When we affirm a child, we offer a firm statement of strong support, but affirmation also gives children strength when they hear it.

To affirm is to make a neutral, judgment-free statement. Its essence is descriptive. An affirmation is powerful and valuable because it is able to encompass the past, present, and future—to endorse and encourage. We do not have to wait for any particular event or achievement to speak out. We can help our daughter to understand who she is at any time by describing what we see—her qualities and personality, likes and dislikes, particular talents—and then confirm how much we enjoy her as she is.

Parents	Teachers

- Think of ways to describe how she thinks and does things that will "firm her up," make her feel confident and strong inside.

  —"I love the way your eyes crinkle at the edges when you laugh."

  —"I've noticed how well you organized everyone to . . . , which makes me think you're responsible enough to go to the mall with friends on the weekend."

- Ask her to help you with tasks either because she is good company or because she's good at that sort of thing.

- "I like your ideas and what you are trying to say. They'd be clearer and more powerful if you separated them. Try writing each idea down and thinking how each links to the rest."

- "Of course you will feel sore that Carl is using the computer before you, but alphabetical order is what the class agreed on."

2 | Appreciate her achievements

You need to believe you can do it.

—Sara, age 10

For a young child, every day brings fresh challenges and fresh achievements. One day she can't do something, yet the next she can. Life is a growing experience in which each day more becomes manageable so competence can blossom. These achievements become the expression of being, and it is essential that they be fully appreciated.

One of the meanings of *appreciate* is to be sensitive to. That is a significant definition. It suggests we should be sufficiently sensitive to see things on her level and in her terms, that is, in relation to her challenges and difficulties, her limitations and capabilities, not our expectations.

Appreciation also includes the notion of value increasing, as in the value of houses or other forms of saving. Each child can be viewed as our most valuable asset. She will see that she goes up in your estimation each time you appreciate her and what she has managed to achieve. Of course, you love her, too, and she remains as important to you as ever, but every child really flies if she feels that those on whom she relies and whom she loves to the bottom of her being believe she has the potential to develop and impress.

Parents	Teachers

- "Achievement" can be very widely interpreted: Any advance in reading level, sociability, math computation, height and reach, ball skills, being able to dress unaided, confidence, learning to swim, pack bags for school or an overnight with a friend can be openly appreciated.

- Appreciation energizes. When girls hear your appreciation, they feel able to move forward. Those who receive little can get emotionally and developmentally stuck and become demoralized.

- Many schools have reward systems that acknowledge achievement for each individual, rather than for what is exceptional in the group.

- Appreciate a wide variety of skills and knowledge, not simply those related to the academic learning on which most lessons concentrate.

- Appreciate, in other words be sensitive to, each child's vulnerabilities. Some may need to hear appreciation more frequently.

3 | Approve of who she is

When I get praise, it makes me feel special.

—Carly, age 8

Approval is the green light to grow, to carry on in the same way because she is good and lovely and fine as she is. Girls need this not only from their mothers, but also—as they enter their preteens—from their fathers if this is feasible. As soon as girls start to fashion their individual identity around being female, from about the age of eight, they benefit from having a mature male who will not just approve of them but also show profound respect to them as they explore ideas of gender differences, what kind of relationship with the opposite sex they might expect, and what being female might mean for them. Male friends, uncles, or cousins or a friendly neighbor may be able to step in where a father is absent. In any case, mothers should be careful not to disparage men in general because girls need to be able to explore relationships with the opposite sex confidently.

But gender is only one aspect of a girl's identity—one of the later spoonfuls of color added to her personality palette. She is already an individual, and she needs to feel approved of for all her strengths, weaknesses, fears, habits, and eccentricities.

Parents	Teachers

Parents

- Hear her side of the story. Assume the best of her, not the worst.

- Let her tell you about her disappointments, and realize what they mean to her.

- Respect her ideas—of what to play or wear; her methods—how to study; and her preferences when these are important.

- Listen to what she has to say, keeping your opinions to yourself unless she asks for them.

Teachers

- Avoid stereotyping. Each girl is an individual, not a replica of anyone, even an older sibling.

- Acknowledge that each student's point of view will be the result of her unique experiences over the years.

- Accept that different children learn in different ways, and be tolerant of each one's preferred style.

4 | Admire rather than adore

When parents put their daughter on a pedestal, it presents her with a very hard act to follow. Most girls would prefer not to have that pressure. The following conversation between a mother and her four-year-old daughter highlights the problem: "I adore you, Susie!" "Don't adore me, Mommy"; "Why not?" "Because I cry too much."

What Susie is trying to say is "It is too much for me always to behave in a way that pleases you and makes you adore me. I know I'm not that good all the time, because I cry a lot, which makes you mad, and I can tell that you don't adore me then."

Adoration is a form of worship, and children don't want to be treated as a god. We may feel it privately, for most of us think our children are a gift from above, but we should express something more measured. We can admire how any girl in our care copes in a particular situation; admire how she manages to overcome her fears or admire how she approaches a problem. She will realize she is in command during these moments and that the occasion is specific. What she certainly cannot directly control are our feelings: These are our business and it is unfair to load her with any responsibility for them. Even when she cries, we should show we love her for being who she is.

Parents	Teachers

- Don't put her on a pedestal. Let her feel special to you because she is yours, but let her feel normal in relation to her peers.

- Show admiration for what she does—"Well done!" "Nice work!" "Interesting idea"—but don't worship the ground she treads on.

- Keep her free of emotional obligations to you: Don't require her to earn your love or behave in a certain way to keep you entranced.

- Teachers are unlikely to "adore" a particular child in their class, but having one or two favorites is quite common. Girls who are vulnerable may interpret not being a favorite as being actually out of favor, which may undermine their willingness to work well with you.

- Try to keep even your admiration in proportion, and always keep it private; at the very least, find some facet in every student that you can respect and admire.

5   Attention is what all girls really want

*When my mom ignores me, I feel like climbing into
bed and crawling under the covers.*

—Amy, age 9

Children need to be noticed. They are very small creatures in a very big world, which is sure to appear huge,
confusing, and even intimidating to them. Our supportive attention fires them up; it gives them the energy and confidence to find their way. Without it, they
can feel lost and as small and insignificant as an ant.

Girls need appreciative attention. When children are
young, they are learning at a speed that would exhaust
most adults. What gives them special pleasure is to gain
greater control of their life and more independence as
they become taller, stronger, more dextrous, and better
coordinated. They can acquire an enormous sense of
pride in their achievements as they reach the top of the
jungle gym, learn to jump into the deep end of the swimming pool, skip with ropes, or simply become sufficiently
tall to open the freezer or reach the faucet or light switch.
At these moments of personal triumph, their whole self
shouts, "Look at me!" If we are absent either physically or
mentally, they could become dejected and crestfallen.

Parents	Teachers

- Remember that attention seeking is usually attention needing. Give your daughter more attention if she starts to pester and irritate, but only when she has calmed down.

- When you are focusing on her, give her your full attention: Don't answer any telephone; don't sneak in a coffee with a friend on your special trip out together; and refer to any special chats or episodes later, so she knows you were paying attention.

- Think of the everyday things you do that she might feel excluded from and ways she could become more involved. She's bound to want to see where you work, for example.

- Girls who don't demand attention are easy to take for granted. They could be simply being "good," having no troubles lurking underneath. But troubled girls often become quiet and may need sensitive attention.

- Identify the girls you have contact with who are quiet or withdrawn. Speak briefly to each of them around school over the next three or four weeks, or just smile and say, "How're things?"

- If a quiet girl is with friends when you think to reach out to her, ask if she has a moment and include a practical issue in the discussion as well as something affirming. She'll then have a safe answer for friends if they ask her what you wanted.

6   Anticipate her problems and feelings

Girls are inclined to be natural worriers, so much so that they can sometimes seem to take on the cares of the world—especially during their early teens, when their moral sense is reaching maturity. They will worry about any difficulties their mom might be experiencing, about their pet's illness, or about problems their close friends have shared with them. They are also far more likely than boys to think ahead and become concerned about any forthcoming pressures or changes in their lives. Parents can help a great deal if they take a moment to try to anticipate their daughter's likely feelings and reactions and offer comfort to reduce the anxiety.

Demonstrate by example and try to anticipate how she may respond to something potentially difficult that is coming up in order to help her prepare. Encourage her to be honest about and reflect on her feelings by chatting about how you felt when it happened to you, or say, "I imagine that was difficult for you." Although we do not want to generate anxiety where none exists, a girl can be relieved to discover someone understands her worry, especially if she has tried to disguise it.

Parents	Teachers

- Anticipate how your daughter might react to something that is about to happen. If she will be distressed or disappointed, tell her you realize this and address the details that may worry her to put her more at ease. She will at least feel accepted and understood.

- Through positive feedback and prompting and through lots of talk that focuses on today's, yesterday's, and tomorrow's events, we can help her anticipate outcomes and become more sensitive to other people's likely reactions.

- Rather than allow her to stay locked safely in the present, help her to reflect on the past and future and make sense of these if they are uncomfortable.

- Try to imagine the particular difficulty a girl who is struggling might confront with a particular assignment. Approach her and acknowledge this, perhaps suggesting a few helpful guidelines.

- Give her faith in her ability to do the assignment well enough in a way that represents a learning advance for her.

7 | Help her achieve her aims

My nine-year-old daughter decided she wanted to re-decorate the dolls' house her uncle had made her. She wanted to stick fresh wallpaper in every room, put new carpets down, hang new curtains, and repaint the front. It was a big project that she could not manage without help to acquire usable scraps of material (that were to color-coordinate) and to cut pieces to size. She was determined to complete the project and did so, with lots of parental input. The valuable lessons she learned were that it is safe to have aims, how to realize and complete a project, and how she could rely on us to help her out.

Girls can be dogged and determined: Their perseverance is generally better than that of boys of a similar age. Their weakness is that sometimes they need things to look and be perfect. They can get angry and frustrated and discard the offending item or piece of work in the trash because flaws—which are inevitable—are unacceptable. They should be assured that, from time to time, good enough works well enough and any high standards can be adjusted.

Parents	Teachers

- Whereas it may be pushy to ensure that a girl will reach the goals we determine, it is wholly supportive and encouraging when we help her identify practical pathways to those she sets for herself.

- Help her to set out a detailed plan that will enable her to achieve her more challenging aspirations.

- Ask her what equipment or help she needs, but don't take over and make it your project.

- It is important that children receive constructive feedback that helps them to learn, to develop their understanding, and, through this process, to learn how to increasingly manage their own progress.

- Girls will be helped to achieve their aims and manage without constant confirmation that they're doing fine when they plan their own work, then carry out their plan, ending with a review of what went right and wrong in order to assess how to approach that same task next time. This is known as *feedback for learning;* in shorthand, plan, do, review, then reframe.

8 Acknowledge her personal strengths

Girls don't have to be "good at" something before they gain our attention and regard. Each will possess personal qualities, inclinations, interests, and strengths that can be noted, appreciated, and—most important—brought to her attention. Praise should always encompass far more than pats on the back for specific accomplishments. Sometimes, an aggressive determination will be her route to achievement, and that style of working should be accepted if that is her way.

If we reflect back and give a name to some of the warmer, caring qualities she demonstrates to us or friends, as well as to those strengths, such as perseverance or determination, that often lead to achievement, she will be able to develop a picture of her whole self, just as she can see her physical self in a mirror. It will help her to value her social qualities and consider these important, too.

The kinds of personal strengths we can acknowledge and encourage in our daughters include thoughtfulness, understanding, willingness to share, caring, forthrightness, curiosity, a sense of humor, a good memory, organization, imagination, the ability to relax, lightheartedness, good powers of concentration, interest in ideas, and good coordination—to name some.

Parents	Teachers
• Acknowledge the full range of your daughter's possible talents and interests.	• Acknowledge that each child is an individual with rights to be heard and respected.
• Acknowledge positive thoughts as well as positive deeds.	• List the personal strengths of any girl whose behavior is causing concern, and make sure she and other children realize you appreciate these.
• Focus on the necessary "doing" aspects of achievement—the inclination to try—as well as the amount she had tried by the end of the process.	• Choose a girl to perform any task that might develop or demonstrate her personal strengths.
	• Take care to balance out your attention sufficiently so an attempt to help one individual does not appear as favoritism.

*Even when I tidy my bedroom and eat all my beans
and mushrooms, my mom never says, "Well done."*
—Puja, age 10

We cannot talk about what we have noticed unless we remain aware of a girl's moods, what has delighted her, her preferences, and so on. We can be with our child all day without really noticing any of these, or we can see our daughter for only two or three hours a day and be acutely sensitive to her body language, expressions, tone of voice, choices, and demeanor.

Being aware does not necessarily mean we should discuss every concern or interpretation then and there, but we would be wise to note it and watch for a possible pattern. Signs of deepening problems could be spending more time in her bedroom, becoming increasingly fussy about food or critical of her own schoolwork, or finding it hard to sleep. Although girls are generally more inclined to be open than boys, older girls especially may clam up following what they see as intrusive questioning about friendship problems. One eleven-year-old said, after her mom contacted another girl's mom about an issue, that she wouldn't tell her mom anything again. Especially after a tiring day at school, children want to relax, remain quiet, and reflect. Any rebuff from your daughter, often done with a curt "fine," is not necessarily an indicator of big trouble she'd rather keep private, but just of the need to be alone in her personal space for a while.

Parents	Teachers

Parents

- Watch discreetly how she relates to her brothers and sisters. Compliment her if she is able to manage any disputes, holds her own without aggression, or ignores being baited by others.

- Make a mental note of which events make her enthusiastic and which tend to make her sad or disappointed.

- Be careful not to seem like a spy: "I have generally noticed/been aware that . . . " or "It's become clear to me that . . . " is better than "I have been watching you from a distance, and I've seen you be really . . . "

- If something important is to happen at school— a test, a notable visitor, a special fun class, a class play—make sure you remember to ask how it went.

Teachers

- It is easy to comment positively on students' work when they hand it in as an assignment but less easy to remark on their wider attitudes and supportive behavior unless you look out for these.

- Be alert for signs of sadness or depression. Sensitivity to these will imply you have bothered to notice and know a student well enough to realize things aren't quite right.

10 Her, not your, aspirations matter most

I've already decided. She's going to be a doctor when she grows up. I've set my heart on it, and I'm going to do everything I can to get her interested in human biology and how the body works as she goes through school!

This single mom had had a hard time and was desperate to give her daughter a better life. She thought that giving her clear aspirations for a stable and successful professional future would be the best she could do for her. Her daughter is still too young to know whether her mother will get her way! It is certainly better that we look hopefully on her future prospects than that we profess doubt and derision, but it is potentially dangerous to be as predetermined as this mom.

Her daughter may, for example, stifle some special interest that develops for fear it could divert events from the path her mom has chosen for her. Or a parent's dream may become obvious, and the daughter may be tempted to thwart it out of spite. She may, though, enjoy following this destiny and see it as a gently amusing game. The most valuable thing we can nurture in our daughters is the confidence, optimism, trust, motivation, space, and self-determination to develop their own aspirations.

Parents	Teachers

- Offer plenty of attention, affirmation, and structure so your daughter has the confidence to imagine herself doing well and the creativity to aspire.

- Help to ground those aspirations in reality by discussing practical plans for making them happen.

- Even small girls will express wishes and desires: "I want to draw a plan of the backyard": "I'd like to play a hospital game when Cara comes over"; "I'd like to play guitar." If you help to make these happen, she will know it is safe to dream and possible to influence her own destiny.

- Help to make her future feel safe and full of potential by creating a secure present.

- Learning should help us all to explore "our possible selves." It should open up possibilities, not close them down.

- Help girls to express their aspirations and narrow down the possible routes to achieving them. After a good piece of work, or a good class, ask where she sees this leading because you see all doors opening for her.

- From a young age girls can be encouraged to think ahead and conceive of what they might do or be as adults, where they might live or what their favored pastimes will be. The future should offer potential, as opposed to being avoided and remaining empty.

Chapter 3

The Basic Principles of Effective Praise

Keeping praise effective is important. There is no point in praising a girl if she is going to end up feeling oppressed or manipulated by our praise or resentful because we have not got it right. Resentful children have a tendency to hit back where it hurts most, so if we show that her performance in basketball or swimming tournaments, in school, or on the stage is the part of her that really matters to us, that could be what she decides to opt out of either to pay us back for our interference or to deflect the constant pressure.

We praise children because we believe it helps them, so there is no point in trying to build a child's confidence if it leads to the opposite: a child with an unstable sense of self-worth who needs regular reinforcement and frequent success to remain convinced of her ability and our approval. It is not to any child's advantage to become so used to praise that its absence can be interpreted as disapproval or disappointment.

The hallmarks of constructive praise are that it should:

Strengthen self-belief. Generalize the achievement where possible and pay as much attention to a girl's capacity to achieve as to the quality of any specific outcome, and be believable. Possible comments are "You're good at *that sort of thing*" or "Now you've done it once, that should give you the confidence to understand it the next time."

Leave her with the possibility and opportunity to change.   Allow her to be different or to do something differently next time. Praise should not, therefore, lock any girl into a single way to please, perform, or do things by being too narrow and focused. Children develop and change as they mature and grow, as adults do, which is one of the potential delights of living for all of us.

Deter dependence.   Encourage her gradually to judge things for herself, by making clear your confidence in her ability to do so and by leaving her in charge of her development. This will also help her to realize that what matters most is the pattern of her personal progress and learning, not the precise outcome on any specific occasion.

It may seem hard to offer enough praise to encourage a child yet avoid the danger of overdoing it, but it is not so difficult if the ten basic principles of constructive praise, set out in the next ten tips, are followed.

11 Let her impress you

A girl loves it when people she respects and admires show clearly and freely that they are genuinely impressed by something she has done. Showing and stating you are impressed is a very effective and straightforward form of praise, which helps a girl to stand more upright, inspired by extra confidence and pleasure.

Being impressed sidesteps the judgment that is implied in so much praise. Most important, it is unconditional. "I am really impressed!" or "That was impressive!" says it all—no ifs and buts to qualify or detract from the message. There is nothing grudging about being impressed, and when girls hear someone say so, they are able to feel appreciated and more confident.

Mothers and fathers who are able to be impressed by their daughter clear the air of competition. Being impressed levels the playing field, as it shows you don't need to prove that you are stronger, better, and more clever. And being impressed doesn't mean a girl has got the better of you in some way or will stop trying. It simply signifies respect and admiration, which is what girls, like boys, thirst for.

Parents	Teachers
• Compare her favorably with you as a child: "I couldn't have managed that when I was your age"; "I wish I'd been able to do that/draw/sing as well as you can."	• "You showed an impressive degree of understanding in that essay."
• "I thought you played impressively well. Were you pleased with what you did?"	• "I'm impressed that this piece of work was so much better laid out. It must have taken you longer, but thanks for giving it extra time. It was worth it."
• When playing any game, let a small child win in little ways, and show you're impressed by her increasing skill.	• "That's an impressive improvement."
• Ask her to help you fix things, organize things, decide things, clean things; then say, "You're terrific at that. You were really useful."	• Give quieter girls responsibilities, such as reporting back on group discussions and looking up information for everyone's benefit. Show how impressed you are by her competence.

12   Make it mean something—be specific

I prefer getting praise from my mom. She explains why it's good or bad, which is much more helpful.

—Annie, age 8

It helps girls to trust their ability where they are doubtful if praise is descriptive and specifically related to a particular piece of work, achievement or action and to a particular aspect of it. Of course, describing something in detail proves without doubt you have noticed your daughter's effort or thoughtfulness, but your observations also help the feedback to be accurate, relevant, and persuasive while having the additional advantage of being nonjudgmental.

It is very common for girls to focus on their mistakes rather than their achievements. Although it is important that girls not shy away from shortcomings or read too much negativity into them, adults must be careful not to say things in a manner that feeds any underlying self-doubt. A girl should be clearly told the root of her success to realize it was not a fluke, so that her self-belief is strengthened. Similarly, any disappointing results should be analyzed with specific reference to techniques, knowledge gaps, and so on, rather then personal weakness.

Parents	Teachers

- Describe in some detail what she's done that is pleasing so she's clear what's right about her approach and what she needs to repeat next time.

- When looking at one of her paintings, discuss the colors used or the size or shape. Ask why or whether she likes what she's done, whether she planned it, or if it just turned out that way.

- Describe what you appreciated about how she behaved after an event rather than comment every few minutes as the occasion unfolds.

- Encourage girls to evaluate each other's work, not to encourage competition but so they may learn from each other, be less secretive, and be more descriptive and less triumphant about what counts as quality.

- Girls need to know in detail what they did right and wrong, so comments and marks should be full and clear as well as encouraging.

- Help a girl to feel it is okay to be proud of good work: "I bet you felt pretty happy with this piece of work. You should."

13 | Keep praise private

You don't like it when they show it off to other people, then everyone looks at you. It's so embarrassing. It's something that should be kept between the parent and child, though I don't mind if my sister knows—she's much older. Sometimes they say it to other parents, who say their child did very well, too, when you know they didn't! It's more moms than dads. They gossip!

—Maria, age 11

Girls are far happier than boys to receive public praise. Perhaps they are more inclined to strive in order to impress others, so they prefer others to know when they succeed. The girls in one single-sex school complained that special achievements—for example, in sporting, academic, or drama competitions—were no longer getting a mention in the school newsletter, and they asked for this to be changed. The desire for public accolades should, though, be limited where possible, because they encourage a dangerous focus on striving for public status instead of a healthier interest in self-improvement and development.

At home, everyday praise should be a private matter between parent and daughter, not paraded as something for any siblings to become jealous of. Bigger achievements should, as a matter of course, be openly celebrated—though you should first check that your daughter is happy with this plan.

Parents	Teachers
• Celebration is a public statement, but everyday praise and encouragement should be private.	• Private praise encourages a safer focus on her personal progress. Public praise may encourage unhelpful competition, tempting girls to work hard for the wrong reasons.
• Ask yourself whose business this is. Usually, it relates only to parent and child, for it is no one else's responsibility.	• If you profile someone's achievement in, for example, an assembly, check afterward whether she was comfortable with the experience.
• Keeping praise private helps to keep it in proportion. The more people you tell, or the more people present when you say it to her, the more it will seem to grow in importance and court unintended consequences.	• Don't forget the parents. Some girls might prefer to have a note sent home rather than their classmates knowing of an accomplishment.
	• Have a quiet word with a student as she leaves the class if you want to say a special "well done."

14   Let her take all the credit

It is often taken as a sign of good teaching or parenting if a child excels, so either adult may seek to claim credit when a daughter, student, or class does well. Of course, we might have had some influence, by reading to her a great deal when she was young, driving her to and from extra classes or training, helping her with her math when she was stuck, encouraging her to keep a daily diary on special holidays, or nurturing any special fascination with botany, astronomy, or breeds of dog that might have livened her mind. But her actual achievement—on the day—is always hers, and it is cruel, selfish, and shortsighted to suggest anything else. If we need to boost our own self-esteem through claiming success on the back of our child's, the most obvious message is that success is something she, too, needs before she can feel acceptable and complete.

In the same vein, if we help in a manner that makes her believe—or means she cannot be sure—that her success was not due to her own efforts only, it dilutes the potential gain in self-belief and confidence, which would be a great pity if she could, indeed, have achieved it on her own.

Parents	Teachers

- Never attribute any of her success to you. Make it clear that she can feel 100 percent it was her work; otherwise, she may feel she needs you next time, too.

- If you find yourself saying, "That homework we did. . . . What was our mark?" realize that you could be about to walk off not only with some of the credit but also with ownership of the work!

- If she refers to your help, make it clear to her that it was she who delivered on the day, and further, that help from you won't always be necessary.

- In the context of standardized tests, it is hard not to claim much of the credit if a whole class does better than expected. Nevertheless, each girl must feel she did it herself, even if she was well taught by you!

- The more detail a girl has about why she did well, the more she can see and believe it was her knowledge, learning, and application that took her there.

15 | Be careful with judgment

When my father came to my dance recitals, he always judged everybody, including me. He said one girl was too fat to dance, another "would grow up to be a stunner." A couple were identified as "the best" (not me), and he said I was a bit stiff. Of course, whenever he attended, I got anxious and stiffened up. I got to be pleased when he couldn't make it.

—Bridget, age 16

My teacher told me I'd got all A's and one "whoops." Well, the "whoops" was a B+. I felt really bad about it, but it really wasn't that bad.

—Elaine, age 10

Children need to be noticed rather than judged. It is fine to evaluate some of what they do, but it is not fine to be judgmental about who they are. When children are young they cannot conceptualize this distinction, so they take all criticism personally and conclude they are in some way bad. They don't want to be evaluated from dawn to dusk, being monitored constantly and required to stay in line. If this happens, girls can develop "learned helplessness," where they continuously demand help to remove the risk of getting something wrong. Children thrive when they are open and feel free within safe limits, not where they are constantly on edge, waiting for the reward or the punishment.

Parents	Teachers

- Be sure that your expectations are age-appropriate: Young girls cannot help being careless.

- Keep shame and guilt out of it. Your daughter will feel these naturally if she believes she has let herself down, but don't set out to make her feel bad about herself because you feel disappointed.

- You bring about what you fear. Girls will flaunt bad behavior if they expect to be reprimanded. It ends the waiting and puts them in control and so is less humiliating.

- Expectations must always be appropriate and criticism reserved for actions that girls can easily change.

- Encourage girls to assess their own work.

- Keep feedback neutral and descriptive rather than either flattering or harsh and negative.

- Shame often encourages girls to ignore or reject suggestions for improvement. Use it very sparingly, if at all.

16   Be truthful, not gushing

It can get annoying if it's said over and over again. Sometimes it's for something really small, like adding something right, and my mom goes on and on about it.

—Lauren, age 8

Even young girls can detect what they might view as "gush and mush"—overenthusiastic adulation that seems unrelated to the effort entailed and was certainly not expected, let alone desired. It is too emotional, too intimate, and may feel especially inappropriate if a girl achieved something entirely to satisfy herself. Gushing praise also encourages a girl to believe that she is responsible for a parent's excessive delight, and that it is your delight that counts. What counts, of course, is her own sense of pride, fulfillment, and pleasure—she must eventually do things to a standard to please herself, not to gain riotous applause from the parental gallery.

False praise is not only offensive and insulting but also does not help any child or young person to develop good judgment. Over time, a girl must learn to judge her effort and work herself. If we go overboard when she knows something could have been done better, she will find it harder to tell what is good enough and what could be improved upon. For any girl who tends to overvalue her work, gushing will be particularly unhelpful.

Parents	Teachers

- Don't pretend, but be positive and upbeat when you can. Make the scope for improvement very clear and encourage her to accept and understand shortcomings: "I don't quite call this a tidied room. You've done well so far, but that pile of magazines still needs sorting. When you've finished, I'll bring you up a soda and admire the room!"

- Point out to her the pleasure she gets, so she learns to perform for her own benefit, not ours.

- Some children need more of a boost and find measured praise hard to believe. However, these girls just need praise more often, not more enthusiastically or exaggeratedly, because they won't believe that either.

- If you are honest but encouraging about the bad, students will be more inclined to believe honestly given praise.

17 | Praise the process, not the product

Many skeptics of the value of praise complain that the quality of the product does matter—and more than the process. What is the point, they argue, in claiming something is good when it is not, and in ignoring the reason—that someone simply did not try hard enough when she could obviously do better?

Naturally, at some point quality does matter, and girls should indeed be called to account if they failed to make any effort. But trying is always valuable: No one makes any progress without some commitment and effort applied to learning more or doing better. Effort, at the beginning, is necessarily often crude and inefficient and the product flawed compared with what we could do, but that is how we all started—and we have survived! Children cannot continuously be told something is not good enough. Effort involves the process, or "doing"; skills such as determination and tenacity need to be valued and encouraged.

Parents	Teachers

- Remember that "process" includes interest, effort, determination, and good work habits, and that these characteristics should all be valued as part of learning and growing.

- Take seriously any effort mark supplied by your daughter's school. Sensitive to her age and stage, schools often judge effort better than parents.

- Young children don't understand what it means to concentrate. Encourage concentration by reading longer stories to your daughter or playing board games that take patience and thought.

- Learning is an emotional activity, so ask if it was hard, if she worried about the outcome, or if she faltered in the middle.

- Through use of the "plan, do, review" model of learning (see Tip 7), children can begin to reflect on working style and learn to judge the effectiveness of their efforts.

18 | Tell it straight and right away

For the best effect, praise should be given straight, with no ifs and buts, no sarcasm, no reminders of past failures or other putdowns to dilute its effect.

And it should be given right away whenever possible as that conveys spontaneity. Sometimes the positive response does not occur to us at the time, or we are busy with other children so don't really take the relevant information in. A parent who is out of town for work should be primed to say something appreciative on the telephone that day rather than wait until the homecoming and receive the lists of good deeds that need complimenting. Most girls would rather hear an informal, more genuine comment at the time (even if that means it is less well informed) than a measured, serious assessment delivered later.

Better late than never is certainly advisable; but even better to say it sooner rather than later.

Parents	Teachers

- Children take praise very seriously, so treat it seriously. As it's not the moment for jokes, don't be sarcastic if you want your comments to be effective.

- If you didn't respond at the time, make amends by saying something like "I thought again about what you told me, properly this time. Sounds like you did really well and it was important. That's terrific."

- Say it as if you mean it, and while you are looking at your child, not as you turn to leave the room.

- The quicker you can give feedback on work done, the more a girl will learn from your comments because she will still remember how she approached the task and can see both what she did well and what she needs to change.

- If you make positive comments on children's personalities, interests, sociability, and style, these can be given immediately.

19 Focus on the achievement, rather than on her

"Focus on the behavior, not on the child" is recommended by most parenting pundits. It is fundamental and is as relevant when praising a girl as it is when reprimanding or disciplining her. Separating children from their behavior makes so much sense in relation to discipline. Letting a child know she's loved—that we're just not wild about what she's done—allows every child to hold onto that all-important sense of self-worth that feeds self-respect and the will to do well.

In relation to praise, we should always focus on what it is our daughter has achieved, not on who she is. "That was terrific, what you managed to do" is far less emotionally entangling than "You're so wonderful to have got that far/done that. I love you so much!" Your daughter may not feel so wonderful, knowing full well that she didn't pull out all the stops for this event. She may realize, too, that you scold her when she has been naughty, so she knows she is not always so wonderful. We should love and feel proud of our daughters all the time and not ration these feelings, reserving them for when they do well.

Parents	Teachers

- Girls under three cannot separate what they do from who they are, so very young girls need it very simple. Approval words that mention the achievement will be enough, such as "Nice try!" "Eating all your dinner was great"; "Great catch!" "Lovely picture"; "Nice job waiting your turn."

- From about age ten, girls feel more emotionally independent. They no longer want much public display of affection because they are trying to be free. Surprise hugs are great, but praise should always commend the achievement, not your daughter: "That was a clever thing to do," not "You are so clever."

- Girls may like to feel liked—as in accepted and enjoyed—by their teachers, but they tend not to relish favoritism or personal comments. "Janie always gives her work in on time" is easier to accept than "Janie's the only reliable girl here when it comes to handing in work."

- "That exercise you did for me last month was great. That shows you can do it," rather than "You're really clever, if only you'd believe it. Of course, you'll do it fine."

20 | Offer good news–bad news choices

I like to hear the bad stuff first, because otherwise it seems even worse.

—Tiffany, age 13

I like the good news first. Then I can take the bad news better.

—Katherine, age 10

There are two parties in any learning situation: the teller and the person being told. To be effective as a mentor, coach, or mere supporter, we have to understand how the information we have to offer may be received. Truth and honesty may be what we're ready to give, but if the girl who receives the "telling" isn't ready to hear it, she can block it by denying or ignoring it.

So if we decide the time has come not to beat around the bush anymore, either because she's now older and may not need so much coddling or because she has started to misjudge herself, we can begin by giving her some control over the level of honesty in any feedback. If we give her the choice of hearing the good news or the bad news first, she's far more likely to remain receptive to the whole message.

Parents	Teachers

- Be sensitive to the moment: Consider the context and recent events. If she's had a tough time and disappointments elsewhere, don't choose that moment to "give it to her straight"!

- If you have not asked her what she thinks, begin your comment, "I think you know this already, but you were a bit slow off the mark at the start/you weren't turning quickly enough . . . " The point is to reduce her dependency on you.

- Always ask at the end, "Did you think my comment was fair?" or "Was it useful to hear that?"

- Check afterward how your comment was received: "I was quite honest with you on that. Did it upset you, or was it helpful?"

- Feedback is a process, and learning is a two-way street. Allow and encourage students to reflect and discuss with you how they react to your style and approach. Listen to class opinions, but note individuals' views, too.

Chapter 4

Ages and Stages:
Adapting to Development

The five separate stages of childhood mark key changes in children's needs, in what they are progressively able to do, how they are able to think, what they are able to understand, and therefore how they will see themselves. It is clear, then, that parents and teachers need to be sensitive to these changes and adjust their praise style and strategies as girls mature.

Newborn babies are engrossed in their physical needs and very dependent for these on their carer. But they also respond vigorously to close attention and react to it very physically—every bit of their body moves, and their whole being seems engaged in the communication. Newborn babies have to face a bewildering array of sounds, smells, signs, and behaviors. The challenge for carers is to make them feel physically and emotionally safe by establishing reliable, close contact and familiarity through regular routines and patterns.

Sometime during the second year, a baby becomes a walking and talking toddler. These skills make her feel far more independent, and her sense of self and gender become clearly established. She will want to explore, experiment, and examine everything. Though she's now capable of doing so much more, her dominant experience may be failure and incompetence as she stumbles and fumbles, breaks things, misjudges things, and tries to make sense of all the rules that suddenly appear.

At this age, girls are generally better coordinated than boys, and their more advanced language skills help them to explain why something happened, but a toddler still needs a great deal of tolerance of the inevitable mistakes made during the steepest learning curve of her life. Encouragement for each small step made toward her self-management and self-control, tolerance of her frustrations, and lots of attention will help her to feel noticed, competent, understood, and affirmed.

From the age of four to about seven, girls see life very simply: Things are either good or bad, right or wrong, which also means that they see themselves in the same simple terms, as either a good girl or a bad girl. Subtlety is not what they're about or what they see, so parents should think carefully about the balance of positive and negative feedback they give. Most of the time little girls are very keen to please, provided they're not angry about feeling left out or being unloved. They still rely on copying—parents, brothers, and sisters—for a lot of their learning, and they need signs of approval that they're on the right track.

In the preteen or "tween" years, girls may need their parents' approval to give them security and confidence as they jump into the shark-filled waters of friendship. Their friends are beginning to matter more to them, and they look to friends for affirmation: Girls this age would prefer to get on with life and not be on constant watch for an adult's approval or disappointment. Tweens are starting to separate, especially from their mothers; are enjoy their growing freedom; and are paying increasing attention to the views of friends. However, they need lots of positive backup as they try out the broader range of skills and activities that their stronger bodies allow. Appreciation of what they can now do is at least as important as approval of who they are at this stage. Sibling rivalry could also begin to focus on a girl's competing talents, so it is important for parents and others to make sure all children feel equally loved and accepted, despite their varying abilities.

Teenage girls still like and value approval, but if praise goes over the top, they feel uncomfortable. They enjoy their efforts being noticed and appreciated, but they are beginning to judge much more for themselves and know exactly how big a deal any achievement is. As one fifteen-year-old said, "My dad's not around much, and when he's here, he's usually reading. I like getting praised by him because he's not really concentrating and it's not gushing, which I like." Another said, "As you get older, you don't need information from parents so much. Your teachers know more what's your level. But it's still good to be appreciated."

One issue with teenage girls is that their increasing independence makes it harder to know what they're doing, good or bad. Any inquisition is likely to feel intrusive and make them retreat into themselves or away from their parents. Their very need for more privacy suggests that they want parents less and more time alone to work things out for themselves.

So lie low, save your celebrations for the notable successes, and in the meantime, focus on affirmation. Make sure, too, that you don't criticize their views and values; their friends, ideas, clothes, and passions; or their creativity—all of which are essential parts of their maturing identity.

21 | Make babies feel safe and secure

Babies are able to read people long before they can read words. They notice and recognize our moods, tone of voice, and physical movements long before they can understand what is being said. They will be more sensitive to these modes of communication than possibly at any other time of their lives, as it is through recognizing patterns in these that they feel linked to our world. Almost from the moment of birth, we know that babies copy as a way to communicate because they can poke out the tip of their tongue when someone does it to them at close range. They let us know how they feel through their limbs, which either flail in distress or twitch excitedly, and, of course, through crying and smiling. Their cries can express hunger, discomfort, loneliness, boredom, or anxiety—any of which an adult might feel. By meeting their need for food, safety, love, warmth, and security, we demonstrate that we understand them and their need for us, which is sufficiently affirming to them so that we can call it praise. What matters to them is less *what* we say than that we say, or even sing, something to them in tones that are familiar and sound soothing. Simply talking, even out of view, tells them that we are near. Paying closer attention and playing with their toes and fingers show that we care and signify that they can rely on us.

Parents	Teachers

- At this age, attention seeking is definitely attention needing. Babies become obviously distressed when someone who is playing with them looks or moves away, and they come alive when adults connect with them directly.

- Choose a song, or make one up, to sing at each clear stage of their day: to mark feeding, bath time, diaper changing, or going to collect an older sibling, for example. The infant will then begin to recognize the tunes and recognize the daily routines.

- Physical closeness— holding and carrying her, playing with her nose or chin, fingers, and toes—establishes and helps her to experience her physical boundaries; this experience provides her first sense of self.

- One-to-one contact with young babies is very important to ground their sense of being, safety, and significance.

- Regular social, visual, and emotional contact and stimulation help their brains to establish positive neural connections.

- Routines are vital to give any baby or young child a sense of safety, order, and security.

22 | Babies must feel they're important

As far as anyone can tell, new babies have very little awareness of having a separate identity: They merge with their caregiver as one. One key way in which they begin to realize they matter to us and develop that sense of being a significant, important and separate person is to have us be in tune with them and responsive to the signals they send out. Psychologists call this form of give-and-take, notice-and-react style of interacting *synchronicity* and *reciprocity*. It is comforting for babies, even at this level, to know that they can communicate and be heard and understood. This is a far cry from the scheduled, overorganized, packaged-up and packed-off babies who are required to fit into other people's superimposed, insensitive, and fixed routines—though it has already been said that babies need some routine.

To reciprocate implies respect for the growing person and her developing personality. This requires that we look, listen and notice, respond, and love and care.

Parents	Teachers
• Allow her to develop her own patterns and pace, and respect these.	• Endeavor to maintain a carer-infant ratio that enables individual infants' patterns to be respected, within a structure that offers familiarity and security.
• Babies work very hard to form an intimate relationship with their caregiver. If we fail to notice their efforts and ignore them, they will soon stop trying and switch off.	• Professional convenience matters, but not if it is acquired at the expense of infant health and contentedness.
• Playing with her fingers, face, and toes; holding her tight and sharing with her the rhythm of our body, as she shares hers with us; and responding to her fears, delights, and sufficiency in relation to food, sleep, or entertainment—all of these activities allow her to sense our deep love and regard for her being and welfare.	

23 Give your toddler a positive view of herself

Toddling girls have a hard time because they make lots of mistakes and have accidents. They can irritate their parents sometimes beyond measure as they try to carve out space for themselves and strive to be listened to in a family's otherwise busy life, often by crying, kicking, and whining. Living with a toddler can be a constant battle, and if it is, it can be a challenge to say enough positive, affirmative, approving, and appreciative things to offset the negative signals we send through shouting, anger, frustration, or simply insisting that our will be done. Yet toddlers need to feel loved and successful to thrive, just like older girls.

Even during the "terrible twos," a girl will not yet have a clear sense of her unique self. She is as she does. When we reprimand her for what she does, applying the behavior-self rule in order to protect her self-respect, she may still feel personally at fault because she is too young to sense or comprehend the difference.

Physical affirmation—that is, plenty of cuddles and close physical contact—will help her get the simple yet strong message of our continuing love and approval.

Parents	Teachers

- Give her plenty of cuddles and physical reassurance, especially after a "bad patch." Don't necessarily talk, or just say, "That was a tough day!"

- Make a joke to end the arguing: How silly we are, fighting like a cat and a dog!

- Toddlers experience themselves through action. Encourage self-management in as many tasks as possible to help a growing girl feel positive about her role in your world.

- Encourage her to dress herself—even if the socks are odd, the T-shirt back to front, or the colors clashing! Involve her in tasks that don't require perfection, such as digging in the yard or decorating cookies.

- Listening helps very young girls to feel they matter. Ensure each one has someone who will hear her point of view.

- When small children are herded, they feel very insignificant.

- Behavior talks: What is she saying? Get to the bottom of persistent bad behavior quickly, before she becomes convinced she is a bad girl.

Until the age of eighteen months, Katie was a model baby. Then, like a typical toddler, she became defiant and disobedient and hated being told no. Katie often flung herself on the floor, kicking and screaming. She would refuse to get out of her car seat. She would scream if I got her drink wrong, in the supermarket, or when I tried to get her dressed and ready to go to my mom's house. Then I decided to pay her more attention, to not be so strict, to let her decide little things, and to play with her more. The improvement was dramatic.

Toddlers are trying because they're trying it on—almost all the time. Having been carried, sat, fed, dressed, driven, and otherwise "done to" all their short lives, they have recently learned they can be a force to be reckoned with. Toddlers use their expanding vocabulary, stronger bodies, and clearer sense of self and purpose to say no and assert themselves—it's an intoxicating power that they use to get noticed, gain some control, and feel important.

But toddlers also struggle with frustration because they can still do so little for themselves. Their ideas race ahead of their bodies, and they confront real rules. Your daughter will feel more grown up, yet she still can't master every task or express complex and powerful feelings with any subtlety. No wonder it's a tough time for everyone involved!

Parents	Teachers
• Don't take your daughter's anger personally. She does not hate you or want to get at you—she's just expressing complex and powerful feelings she can't put into words.	• Offer chances for girls to play through their frustrations, to dance, bash on saucepans, or splash paint on big sheets of paper.
• Express her frustrations for her: "It must have been hard, being ignored/wanting me to stay with you when I had to leave/being fed up with being told what to do and when to do it, when you felt like staying home and playing."	• Choose stories to read that represent girls' difficulties, so they know they're not alone and feel more understood.
• Explain to her older brothers and sisters why she feels so mad and why that can make her a nuisance to them.	
• Make it clear whenever you can that you know she's not being bad, just finding life hard at the moment.	

25 Understand what a schoolgirl can't understand

Most arguments between parents and children happen when children fail to match up to parental expectations. Older children may choose to play in a rock band rather than follow Mom or Dad into the favored family profession, but clashes with young children usually occur where children cannot (or don't) think or behave in the way their parents expect, when they are consequently considered thoughtless, selfish, immature, or even spiteful.

Girls between four and seven or eight are not, and cannot be, grown up. Children develop slowly and in set ways, and some girls develop more slowly than others. "Don't be such a baby!" is especially humiliating if girls have picked up that they should be more reliable, organized, and cooperative and less emotional than they are capable of being. Praise should not be conditional on their understanding more than they can. And criticism should not fly when we are frustrated that they fail to think ahead, understand a complicated rule, anticipate consequences, or imagine how we or anyone else will react. Girls of this age are still very self-oriented: They understand others through assuming others will feel and act as they do, yet their self-understanding is still very underdeveloped.

Parents	Teachers
• When a girl is criticized for falling short, she can easily feel guilty for letting you down and assume there is something wrong with her.	• Girls can find it harder to fit in and participate in class activities if their home life is stressful. Give any temporary "loner" a special buddy, or use paired activities for a while in class rather than larger group ones.
• She has to be very grown-up and organized at school, so she may want to regress after a trying day and be less responsible and more dependent at home. Acknowledging this will demonstrate empathy and understanding.	• If you feel unsure about the key changes that accompany developmental stages for younger girls, consider taking a course or find a suitable textbook.
• Find as many ways as possible to spend and enjoy time with her.	
• Whatever she believes you think of her tends to be how she views herself. If she knows you enjoy her company, find her fun, reliable, and capable, she will work and make friends more confidently.	

26 Help her to see who she is

Early childhood is when a girl begins to fill out her idea of who she is and what makes her unique. By the time she reaches seven or eight, she will have developed a much clearer sense of what she is good at, what her main likes and dislikes are, what and how she prefers to play, how her parents and other adults react to her, and whether she generally attracts praise or provokes anger or frustration.

Parents can help a girl to clarify and deepen her identity and ensure that it is positive. Instead of simply saying, "I think you're lovely!" we can be far more specific and say, "You are really lovely because you are fun to be with, you are very kind to your friends and share things, you love to paint—even though you hate the cleaning up after, you clearly prefer to learn by trying things out rather than just accepting what you're told. . . . " The more detail we can give, while remaining as nonjudgmental as possible, the better she will understand and appreciate herself.

Parents	Teachers

- Make your daughter feel she belongs to a clear family grouping and to you. Arrange family outings and events, tell her about her life as a baby and about what your own life was like as a child, and involve her in as many of your commitments as is practical or sensible.

- Experiment with the concept of a "personality palette." The more patches of color representing different aspects of her personality, skills, and preferences you can help to create and place on her personal palette, the more attractive, colorful, and detailed will be the picture she can draw of herself.

- Make sure each child is aware of something—her special passion or a particular skill—she can feel positive and proud of that will help her to have a clear and positive sense of who she is and her capabilities.

- Help her to be aware of her personal preferences, which will include her preferred working style and her favored activities and subjects. Cover, too, her favorite food, animal, television program, and so on.

27 | Encourage your preteen's developing skills

When my mom asks if I've learned anything new at my gymnastics class, I can't answer because she doesn't understand anything about it. I wish she knew more.

—Melanie, age 10

The preteens, or tweens, are renowned as the five years in which children's confidence typically flourishes, as long as peer or school pressures do not grind them down. Tweens' stronger bodies and more capable minds enable girls to view things more reflectively, to be more determined to master complex physical and mental tasks, and to work out how to correct mistakes when they get things wrong. They move from manipulating things physically to being able to manipulate and reposition them mentally, in their heads, so they can make better sense of instructions about sporting or musical technique and often progress by leaps and bounds.

As girls' physical coordination improves in the tween years, they become far more skilled with their hands. It is the age when they can begin to make clothes for their dolls or soft toys, enjoy braiding friends' or dolls' hair, color in fine geometric grids to create their own patterns, and cut paper more finely and decoratively. It is, typically, the "artsy-craftsy" period. Of course, they can also climb trees and catch, kick, and hit balls better, but for many it is the fine motor skills that they enjoy and develop. Feeling more confident about who they are, preteen girls love adults to notice their skills and maturing sense of judgment.

Parents	Teachers
• Admire your daughter's growing competence so she feels proud and capable.	• Skills that can be applauded and encouraged could include artistic, humor, dramatic, academic, social, communication, sporting, manual dexterity, personal organization, imagination, physical coordination, musical, memory, listening, sound judgment, and empathic skills.
• Give her chances to demonstrate and develop her newly-acquired skills. Ask her to help you with practical and decorative tasks, and appreciate her contribution.	
• Watch her doing something she enjoys, even if it is something you find tedious.	
• Let her be outside and active as much as possible, provided you have gone over appropriate safety rules.	

Accept your tween's need to act female

My nine-year-old daughter suddenly developed an interest in really feminine things and wanted to cozy up to her friends' mothers who fit this stereotype, rejecting me. From having been quite a tomboy, she wanted pretty dresses, girlie toys, and nail polish. I was quite upset, being a strongly committed feminist and working mom who wasn't interested in fashion and the like. I seemed to lose her, then, but by the age of fifteen she became a fighter like me, supporting all the same causes!

Gender awareness flourishes in the tween phase between eight and twelve years of age. Girls gradually pull away from their exclusive emotional need for their mothers as friends rise in significance. Indeed, they explore a variety of female models and stereotypes with their friends; hence the common obsession with celebrity beauties. Their play and interests become very gender-focused, and they look down on boys as subhuman beings.

Preteen girls typically gather in small cliques and talk endlessly. They use their sharper tongues and growing verbal confidence to flatter and suck up to their peers; they also sometimes turn hostile and bitchy to pull rank.

Parents	Teachers

- Try not to criticize your daughter's girly veneer continuously. She is simply "trying femininity on for size."

- Maternal praise may be less powerful while she's trying to separate; paternal praise could matter more.

- Tweens need to demonstrate their difference. By understanding her cheeky challenges, you show you approve and accept her.

- Provided she's not endangered, don't "diss" her friends or any close female role model who is helping her into womanhood.

- While they flirt with femininity and fleeting fashions, comment favorably on tween girls' passions and purpose, to indicate that these inner, personal characteristics remain important.

- Appreciate preteen girls for who they are: growing people who are desperate to fit in and be accepted. Bossiness often hides deep vulnerability and fear of failure.

29 Teenage girls like praise that is measured and moderate

I like them to say something simple like, "Well done. You deserve it." Nothing over the top.
—Hannah, age 16

It can get annoying if it's done over and over again.
—Joyce, age 15

Teenage girls still want to hear praise, but it is better to keep it measured and moderate, to avoid the danger of praise dependency and encourage independent working. They are becoming more discriminating and want you to be honest in your praise. They certainly don't want to be flavor of the week one day and in the dog house the next. What teenage girls appreciate most is being noticed and treated as a source of authority about their welfare, future, and progress. They need to be trusted before they can fully trust their individual ability to evaluate accurately and therefore do well.

Teenage girls value praise and appreciation more when it is sparing. From parents and teachers alike, they report that when praise is in plentiful supply, its value decreases. At this stage, girls say they like their parents to be around at home in the background, to provide a sense of stability—and to chat about this and that if the moment seems right.

Parents	Teachers
• Always ask your daughter how she rates her own work, result, or performance before *you* expound: "That seems like a good outcome/result, but it's how *you* judge and see it that matters more."	• Girls enjoy all of a teacher's commendations—they like to be liked—but those that make the most impact will be directed at her hard work and progress.
• Ask her if the news is worth passing on: "Do you want to contact your dad, or is it not such a big deal?"	• Ensure that any favorable comments are well supported with detail so she knows exactly what it is she has done well and she can believe it.
• Keep it simple: "Well done"; "That's terrific. Were you pleased?"	• For praise to be truly empowering, it must suggest that she has mastered the process just as much as the individual task at hand: "You have written a very good essay. You are planning your arguments much better. Your conclusions are more complete, and you are now weighing different approaches. Great."
• Say something at the end of the week rather than every day.	
• Appreciate her views and values more than her daily results so you seem truly interested in and impressed by her rather than obsessed with what she can do.	

30   Give her faith in her future as an adult

Her parents considered her brilliant, but the better she did in sports, music, and academics, the more she realized there were others who were superior, and she felt like a failure. At college, though she qualified for one of the best, she doubted every assignment and thought she would flunk; it was the same during her professional training and her first year with an employer. Though she aimed high with great results, she could not accept that she deserved her success and that it would continue.

Girls are, by and large, doing well. Self-esteem questionnaires show girls at their lowest ebb at the age of thirteen but with rising confidence from then on, unlike boys, who live on chutzpah and bravado through childhood and reach their low point at the age of nineteen, when they can no longer pretend. But there are still too many girls who lack confidence and can't quite believe they have the qualities that will allow them to go far when they face tougher competition.

Parents can help by commenting favorably on their daughter's growing maturity and general competence, on her time management and problem-solving skills, rather than continuing to highlight specific test scores that make the success fleeting and possibly unconvincing.

Parents	Teachers

- Understand the continual uncertainty your daughter may face.

- Make her believe her destiny is in her hands: "Just look at your past. You're clearly capable of getting to wherever you decide to go. The future is yours. And whatever path or career you decide on, we'll back you."

- Show respect for her ideas, plans, views, and values, and assume that others will respect her, too. Ultimately, these will be more powerful survival tools than her final grades or SATs, so reduce the heat on these.

- Encourage teenage girls to look and plan ahead. Commend their past achievements, and be positive about any future intentions.

- Invite previous high school graduates to return to describe their personal journeys.

- Mentors can help enormously to boost individuals' confidence and focus on the possibility of a brighter future than might otherwise be assumed.

Chapter 5

What to
Notice and Encourage

It is good practice to find at least three things about our children to notice and comment on positively every day, and we should use that comment to point to the past, the present, and the future. You should not be asking *if* a child is good at anything, but "What is my child good at?" because it is undoubtedly true there will be something about what she says or does to notice and appreciate. We just have to be thoughtful and creative.

It is often said that it takes four "praises" to undo the negative impact of one criticism, so how often we should say something encouraging and endorsing depends in part on how critical we have been. Clearly there needs to be a limit: If we say five hurtful or undermining things in one day, then to try to say twenty positive statements that same day to even those out becomes logistically difficult (because we don't necessarily spend that much time together), will be very confusing for our daughter (because we seem to be blowing hot and cold), and can create an atmosphere that is far too intrusive and contrived (because we have to watch so carefully to spot when to pop in the praise). The older girls become, the less they need or want wall-to-wall praise, though of course it still pleases them when they hear it. Encouragement will become more necessarily context-bound, for example, focused on a time of particular challenge. Provided we don't lay it on too thick, girls will come to value these less frequent endorsements and appreciations more highly. Don't forget, though, to continue to say how much you enjoy her company and love who she is. The world ahead of her can seem challenging, even frightening, and she'll need every ounce of confidence she can muster.

There is a vast range of possible attributes and achievements to notice. If we focus on a single area—for example, school grades and work—we have to ask about these every day in order to know what to say. And whichever aspect of her life we notice most could become the part of her she feels we value most, and the one she would choose to sabotage if she ever felt sufficiently angry to want to hurt us.

If we pride ourselves on offering a tolerant, warm, and accepting home, we will value, notice, and openly appreciate all aspects of each child's personality—fears and foibles as well as robustness; skills and talents; general capability; attitude toward others; and the ability to deal with problems.

Appreciate her thinking skills and opinions

It was an interschool debate on some aspect of history in the curriculum that all students present had been studying. The girls who volunteered to participate were so often timid and hesitant, found it hard to stand tall and straight, and were generally unconvincing, even though we had all prepared well. The boys, by contrast, oozed confidence and presented their arguments boldly. They made you believe them. When our history teacher pointed this out, we all had to agree she was right.

—Rachel, age 17

Thinking before acting comes more naturally to girls; they are generally better at thinking ahead, considering consequences, and understanding emotions, all of which helps them to anticipate how others—friends, parents, or "victims"—will react. Girls, though, particularly when they get older and when they're in the company of boys, are reluctant to shape these thinking skills into firm opinions backed by clear arguments. Perhaps because they have had more experience of being considered "good" and have basked in that glory, they are less ready to chance a challenging point of view, delivered with confidence, with which others may disagree. Yet this is a quality all girls need to nurture if they are to make their mark in their adult working life.

Parents	Teachers

- Encourage your daughter to voice opinions. Chat about recent hours or days, and recall what has happened that she might have found fun, scary, or difficult: "It's interesting you've mentioned that. Why did you find it scary?"

- Invite her to plan and think ahead when there's free time to fill or there's an unfamiliar situation to face.

- Value her choices: "That's a good idea of what to play!" "I like how you put that sweater and those pants together."

- Encourage girls to speak out and feel confident in doing so: Ask questions such as "Is there anyone here who likes to solve problems?" and "Let's have another point of view on this. Don't be shy. All views count!"

- Write encouraging comments on each girl's work: "I very much liked your ideas about what Jodie was really thinking in that story."

- Ask her how she would have liked a story or game to end, to stimulate flexible thinking and ideas.

32 Encourage sociability and standing up for herself

Girls are natural talkers and seek more intimate friend-ships so are thought to be better adjusted socially and less likely to be loners. The research tells a different story, for one study showed that one in seven children (girls and boys) thinks he or she has few or no friends. It is also true that successful and genuine friendships demand some very sophisticated skills that don't al-ways come naturally. They certainly benefit from being oiled and practiced at home.

There is a difficult balance to be struck, between girls' learning to accommodate, compromise, be flexible, and respect other people's points of view, all of which aids friendships, and being able to stand up for themselves—not always going with the flow simply to prove member-ship and loyalty.

Social and friendship skills start at home. If we show our daughters respect, talk to them frequently, and give them plenty of time and attention, they will be assured not only that their views matter but also that they are liked, so others should like them, too. And if we ignore our daughter's complaints and disagreements, she'll be less likely to challenge friends when they are embark-ing on risky behavior.

Parents	Teachers

- Value a range of skills that will help her in social situations, such as empathy, understanding, kindness, sharing, and managing arguments without exploding and storming off.

- Expect that she join you sometimes when you visit friends and relatives.

- Try to have at least one family meal each week to encourage conversation and friendly banter.

- Girls enjoy group work, but sometimes they can use it to shirk accountability and find it comfortable that they're not required to defend a personal view. Both styles of learning—individual and group—should be part of any structured learning process to benefit both girls and boys.

- Groups of both mixed genders and the same gender help girls and boys to appreciate each other's strengths and learn from each other.

33 | Acknowledge that she tried hard

Did you try hard and do your best? That's what matters.

Acknowledging effort is always valuable, for progress is made at every stage on the learning journey. The road there is at least as important as arriving, and each arrival point becomes a past staging post from which the learner moves on. It can represent a bigger step forward for someone to realize finally what she's been doing wrong and work out for herself how to correct it than to get something right at the first attempt, but with little awareness of why it was correct.

Effort is important. No one achieves anything significant without it. Effort involves concentration; it means you give it your all. Young children find it hard to concentrate, and they will probably have a poor appreciation of what "trying hard" actually means. But if a young girl's more limited efforts are not respected and valued, it may be harder for her to make the necessary effort when she's older, when she has more control over it, and when the results might matter more.

Parents	Teachers

Parents

- Ask your daughter what she means when she says, "But I tried really hard" before you condemn this statement as a weak excuse.

- Ask for specifics such as how much time was spent on a project; how much time was spent on any diversion, such as TV, the computer, or phone calls; whether she took the time to look something up if she wasn't sure; and whether she left herself time to check over her work.

- If you have every cause to trust her and she says she did her best, not knowing how to do it differently, let it rest at that.

Teachers

- Do you encourage your students to understand what the terms *effort* and *trying* mean?

- Do you talk about how difficult it can be to persevere and what students think and feel when they get despondent? Ask anyone who finds a way through when discouraged to describe what he or she does to achieve this.

Organization matters but "good enough" is also okay

I don't mind that the boys' work is messy or not very fluent, provided they have shown they understand the content. It's the girls who worry me when they underline headings in different colors and make their work pretty as a picture. It's such a waste of their time and so unnecessary. They need to relax a bit.

—High school science teacher

Girls tend to be more responsible and self-organized at a younger age than boys, but the danger is that they may attach too much importance to being neat and tidy and correct in pursuit of being "good" or even perfect. In the long run, girls develop a healthier attitude toward work and themselves if they can let go and trust that they won't be judged as a person by any particular piece of work. They should avoid investing their self-worth in each and every assignment.

If poor personal organization becomes a genuine handicap, we can comment favorably on any small example of organization and self-management. Tidying just a corner of a bedroom is progress; returning for an item remembered at the last minute is better than forgetting it; and prioritizing commitments on a busy Saturday shows forward thinking.

Parents	Teachers
• Suggest strategies to aid your daughter's self-organization, such as making lists or writing reminders on sticky notes.	• Discourage pristine and pretty work, even though it may be easier to read. Homework should be functional, not a time-consuming work of art.
• Ask her how she prefers to remember things. It must become her project, not yours, or it may not work.	• A focus on metalearning—learning how to learn—will automatically encourage girls to consider how they work and the trade-offs between time spent preparing work perfectly and having some fun or learning more things.
• If it is her way to get everything together at the last minute and it works, that's good enough.	
• Better to applaud any developing skills than exude frustration over how far she still has to go. She may be organized in some spheres, just not in the ones you'd like!	• Teach girls the 80:20 rule—that making something 20 percent better often requires 80 percent more time, which is not time-efficient; 80 percent of quality is usually achieved in the first 20 percent of time spent.
• Beware: A heavy emphasis on tidiness could hamper creativity.	

35 | Value her imagination, however fanciful!

I'm a famous dancer. Everyone wants to come to watch me leap and twirl. But one day I fall onstage and hurt myself so badly that I go dead white and lie as if dead. Someone in the audience jumps down from the balcony to try to revive me, using special powers. He gives me a magic kiss and I come to life again. He falls in love with me immediately, and I dance across the stage with joy!

—Kate, age 7

A girl's imagination represents her. It is her own personal creation and gives her not only a sense of freedom but also some productive control over her time. Fantasy allows endless possibilities: She can explore the rare experience of feeling powerful because she can create stories in which she takes a lead role and she has unlimited strength. When she is in charge of the story, nothing can go wrong for her unless she wills it, so she can feel totally safe. If we join in on her terms and accept the role she wants us to play, in effect she is in charge of us, too, which will help her to accept our bidding much of the rest of the time.

Fantasy encourages mental flexibility and creativity, and both help later with schoolwork. We should appreciate and value her ability to draw, play, and explore imaginatively and occasionally play with her, entering her fantasy.

Parents	Teachers

- Don't devalue any imaginative play. It is part of your daughter, gives her great skills, and increases her self-knowledge and confidence.

- Girls explore imagination through fiction and fantasy. At the start they play school, then may reenact stories from adventure books or television series, and later imagine themselves in liaisons.

- If you join in an imaginative game of hers, don't suddenly talk about the shopping you need to do or what she'd like for a snack, as this interruption will shatter her creation and belief that you take her seriously.

- Fanciful imagination can become distracting, but girls need to be able to be themselves and should be encouraged to take risks with possibilities.

- Girls' imagination sometimes appears in the form of humor or silly pranks. To keep it contained, try to find clear times when students are able to play imaginatively with ideas, and allow them to edge toward naughtiness.

36 | Enjoy her humor

Humor is a chief joy in life. Around the age of seven or eight, something very important happens to the way children's minds work. They can look at themselves from the outside, think in abstract categories far more easily, and play with ideas and see new links. Any parent of a girl of this age will tell you that it is at this time they constantly get asked to laugh at what are usually, to begin with, very bad jokes that their daughter considers utterly hilarious. Children's joke books tend to be pitched at this age group. Seven- and eight-year-olds often tell jokes, often picked up from the school yard, that they cannot possibly understand or find genuinely funny, yet they find an alternative explanation that makes sense to them. But it's not just the jokes themselves they enjoy; they take great delight in entering that hitherto closed adult world of telling jokes and being in the powerful position of making other people laugh. They become, in effect, the family's very own court jester.

Once we laugh, the show can go on, and on, and on. It gives her huge pleasure to entertain in this way and makes her feel so proud. We must play the appreciative audience and allow her to exercise her new mental muscles and have fun playing with ideas and words.

| Parents | Teachers |

- Be patient, and try to laugh—or groan—when you are told a joke, even if you have heard it plenty of times before.

- Magic tricks are visual jokes that play with the viewer's perceptions and expectations. Encourage any interest in magic, and be tolerant of the performance that accompanies the performance she may want to arrange for the family.

- From the age of eight or so, children can begin to understand the real humor of jokes and enjoy telling jokes and making them up. Girls' humor should be valued and brought out, even if it is the boys in the class who hold the stage most of the time. Of course, everyone needs to learn that there are good times for being silly and times when it needs to be vetoed.

37 Welcome creativity—and the risks and mess involved

Every human being has the capacity to be creative. Young children find it easiest, because they have less idea of what is expected or what is right and wrong. For them, experimentation is fun and helps them to feel in charge and powerful—free from rules and other restrictions. They have not yet absorbed gender-related social conventions, so all can be encouraged to try out a wide range of activities.

When children express their creativity in less organized ways, we should not devalue it simply because it seems to lack purpose. Building outdoor camps, playing hairstyles with generously adorned dolls, creating dance routines, or making up rules for a variety of games are all creative pursuits.

Creativity is the expression of originality: It helps children to discover their identity and experience directly the ways in which they are unique.

Parents	Teachers
• For girls who are artistic, offer plenty of opportunities to carry on drawing, coloring, painting, and sculpting for as long as they wish.	• Children need peace and quiet to become absorbed in something creative. Try to limit the chat as they explore their ideas, and discourage boys from teasing girls' often more thoughtful efforts.
• Cooking can be very creative; sewing, knitting, crocheting, or gardening can be the basis of many creative productions. Many girls express creativity through pinning up posters and photographs in bedrooms or through painting lampshades.	• Cleaning up afterward helps to instill good organizational habits and encourages a sensible allocation of time. Invite students to gauge how much time is needed.
• Collage-style pictures can be created from discarded trash, fabric swatches, or dried food or from twigs, leaves, petals, and plant seeds.	

38   Go deep—endorse her values and beliefs

If one purpose of praise is to make a girl feel good about who she is inside rather than rely on a range of external shows of such things (clothes, toys, talents) to make her feel comfortable with herself, we need to respect her values and beliefs.

Younger girls will not have developed any consistent system of values for us to appreciate, but they do attach great importance to their friendships and their play. They also possess a natural, passionate concern for fairness that we ignore at our peril. Their beliefs are manifested in the sense they make of their immediate world: These beliefs form the structure that creates coherence when they face and have to manage confusing events.

From eight or so onward, girls' ability to think in more abstract and conceptual ways and see things from other people's standpoint encourages many of them to latch onto concerns that focus on others. Whether it is religion, vegetarianism, the developing world, or animals, we should endorse each girl's right to develop her own values and interests and should respect her beliefs.

Parents	Teachers

- Girls typically develop passions that are more "touchy-feely," unlike boys' more fact-based passions. A girl's passion may include boy bands, horses, drama, dance, or books that involve particular characters. Show interest and help her to find out more to endorse her choices and values.

- If she develops a passion for animals, it means she cares for creatures that need to be looked after. We should respect this tenderness.

- Try to find out about individual students' passions and values, and make reference to these respectfully.

39 Appreciate and develop practical competence

Growing children feel great pride each time they conquer something they were not capable of achieving previously. They spend so many years dependent in some way or other that they have a sense of freedom and autonomy when they grow tall enough, strong enough, dextrous enough, and responsible enough to manage themselves or undertake tasks that combine skill and knowledge and that can help others.

Spatial skills—seeing how things fit together, being able to rearrange objects in their minds and remember routes, maps, and blueprints easily—are boys' forte, but girls benefit from being able to think in this way, too. When a girl is ready, encourage her to read the map while you are traveling somewhere, teach her to play games such as chess, and show her how machines work and how to handle electrical appliances safely.

Practical skills help a girl to manage on her own, valuable not so much for survival but because autonomy is the ultimate expression of self. Competencies, then, help to define and express our sense of self and boost self-esteem.

Parents	Teachers

- Write down all the things your daughter is good at and likes to do. Think of ways you could put any of these skills to practical use in the home.

- If she is too young to be of genuine help, encourage her to come and hold things for you or to pass things to you, and she will learn at the same time.

- Give her any discarded bit of electrical appliance or other equipment (if safe) when it has broken to take apart and explore.

- When a student mentions something she has done, made, or mended at home, compliment the skill involved: "Sounds like you're good at that sort of thing. Want a job in my house!?"

- As girls develop their manual dexterity, show how it can be put to practical use: "Wow. That would make you good at electronics/tuning my guitar/dicing vegetables/ getting my baby daughter dressed in the morning!"

40 | Go deeper—accept her fears and feelings

> *When a child cannot be sad or lonely or angry because her parents will not be pleased with her if she is, she will feel she cannot be the person she knows herself to be, and she will believe that she is unsatisfactory.*
>
> —Dorothy Rowe, author and psychotherapist

A child whose fears and feelings are ignored or denied will not only feel misunderstood but also very alone. Apart from our psychological inheritance, it is our feelings that make us who we are and give us our sense of self. We experience feelings, often intensely, before we have the vocabulary to describe them, and they are our first building blocks. That certain things interest, upset, frustrate, or hurt us; give us pleasure; or make us defensive and selfish—these things create our individuality. If we can recognize all a girl's particular moods and characteristics, we will demonstrate a deep understanding of her and how she sees her world.

When we accept her dilemmas at her level, she will be spared the pain of isolation and the grief of having apparently lost her parents' support. She will be free to be and grow—nothing less.

Parents	Teachers

- Accept that your daughter's fearful beliefs are real to her. She should not be told, "Girls don't believe that nonsense and should not feel scared of things like monsters, the dark, or deep water."

- Notice her happy moods from her body movements, shining eyes, or bouncy walk, and say, "You seem very cheerful today. Something nice must have happened. Lucky you!" and let her keep it to herself if she doesn't want to tell you.

- Notice her sad moods, too, and accept that she will feel angry, jealous, resentful, or lonely or even hate you, and tell her that's natural and okay. Never deny her difficult feelings.

- Many girls are very sensitive and squeamish. Prevent other children in the class from picking on anyone and teasing her for her natural feelings.

- Learning can be frightening. Accept that some reluctance to try could mask a deep fear of failure, and try to get to the bottom of this. The learning environment must be made safe for girls who lack confidence.

- Fears and feelings—indeed, all strong emotions—make learning difficult. Understand what a girl might be going through in her personal life, what pattern and expectation of relationships she brings into school, and consider how these may affect her.

Chapter 6

The Language of Praise:
Ways to Say It—and Give It

Human beings communicate in many subtle and less subtle ways. We use words, touch, facial expressions, and a range of different physical and symbolic gestures. We often merely sense the pleasure we have given others through the tone of voice they use or the way they look at us. We often interpret a number of reactions and piece together an overall impression. As adults, we don't always need to have praise spelled out every time someone feels we have done well.

If praise is valuable and worthwhile because it helps girls to feel acknowledged, noticed, approved of, valued, accepted, and appreciated and helps them to be successful, it follows that there are many ways to bring this about. So it must be the case that praise does not always have to be given in words. As they mature, girls will appreciate the more subtle signs and know we are grateful. Although language is what we tend to use to express our delight, pleasure, and surprise when a child has done well, by extending our praise repertoire we will limit the dangers already noted associated with spoken praise, and we will sometimes surprise them, which is always fun!

Children thrive when they are sure we enjoy their company, so it is important to have fun with them when they do well. We should not make fun of praise or make fun of them by being sarcastic when giving praise, but the whole family can have plenty of fun discovering different ways to express love and appreciation and finding approaches that are lighter in tone.

Keep approval simple

It's nicer if they say lots of different things, not the same thing over and over. And you like it said with expression, so they seem really interested.

—Riya, age 9

The more we spell it out, the more labored, false, inappropriate, or overdone praise can become. To prevent a child's feeling burdened or uncomfortable and even misunderstood by our outpourings we should, quite simply, keep our expressions of approval simple.

Approval, as has been explained, focuses on the individual. It puts the child in the spotlight, which is why she may squirm if it becomes exaggerated. Appreciation, on the other hand, relates to the task and therefore sometimes needs to be more detailed and specific (though still not disproportionate) so our child knows she can trust our appreciation.

Even praise that describes and reflects back what has pleased us (sometimes called *descriptive praise*) can be kept simple if we say things such as "Nice bike riding," "Great catch," or "Well tried," instead of "That was clever, how you biked that tight circle." Leaving some detail out allows her to decide for herself what it was that was good and makes her less dependent on our assessment and freer to make up her own mind.

Parents	Teachers

- Vary the words, style, and response to avoid sounding like a stuck record. Children very quickly switch off and imagine the rest once they hear the intro, especially when we nag. Even repetitive praise gets to sound stale.

- Try such responses as "That's lovely!" "Brilliant!" "Well done!" "That's great!" "Thanks for doing that"; "That was sensible"; "How thoughtful!" "What a great idea!"

- If your daughter begins to look at you askance instead of beaming with pride, go easy. Save your comments for something that matters more to her.

- Comments on written work need to be full and explicit, but spoken approval can be short: "I really liked that story/your arguments/ the line you took. Take a look at my comments."

- Warmer tones of voice and full-hearted attention convey approval, too.

When my mom smiles at me, I kind of know.
—Melissa, age 9

Sometimes children don't need to hear anything spoken. Beaming smiles are often enough. When they reach the finish line in the school race and turn round to see if we saw their effort or their triumph, a smile and a nod from a distance is all we can give—and it is often more than enough.

Parents	Teachers
• We can use commercially available smiley-face stickers sparingly, as a surprise or reminder of our love especially at times we cannot be there. But make no mistake: These will be no substitute for the real thing!	• Smiley faces drawn or stuck on the end of work show you are pleased with the result, but they don't offer useful, detailed feedback when that is more appropriate.
• For a younger girl, we can draw a simple smiley face on a small white board or blackboard in her bedroom after bedtime for her to find on waking. But beware forgetting to do so if it has become a nightly routine.	

43 Talk with touch

Touch has its own language. It can say so much in such a variety of ways, and it need only be fleeting. Touch is, for example, an intimate way to demonstrate an equality of regard and respect. It can express feelings more quickly than words, and although it is less precise, it has the great advantage of allowing the receiver to read what she wants—and needs to hear—into it. It is therefore more likely to hit home and satisfy. Touch is certainly less open to misinterpretation than streams of worthy words and is an important gesture of approval, appreciation, and giving. Its capacity to convey understanding makes it also serve as a useful way to demonstrate empathy.

A child who lives around adults who never touch her, even if they say the "right" praise words, could feel ignored, unworthy of attention, inferior, misunderstood, and, eventually, ashamed—the very opposite of what we hope praise will achieve.

Parents	Teachers
• Experiment with little touches of appreciation instead of using words.	• Of course, it is not usually appropriate for professionals to touch students, especially as they get older. Nevertheless, if you stand quite close while you look over work, you can show you find a girl acceptable and feel comfortable in her presence.
• If touch has disappeared from your relationship with your growing daughter, sit close to her as she watches TV, ruffle or stroke her hair when she comes in from school, or take her hand and play with it as you chat with her at bedtime.	
• If she finds your approaches difficult, ask her before you do it so you know she feels ready for it.	• Consider whether either shaking a girl's hand or giving her a high five is an alternative acceptable way to demonstrate approval and appreciation.

44 Use fun gestures

When my daughter got all A's on some important exams, I made her a special celebratory lunch that consisted only of food beginning with the letter A. There was asparagus soup, avocado pear, some roasted artichoke hearts, apricot yogurt, an apple slice, and almonds. I set her the task of identifying the theme. She thought I was crazy, of course, but she appreciated the gesture!

Money is not the only way to measure value or express pleasure, though it can be very easy to sign checks. Although girls love to get something new that they have longed for, they also appreciate being on the receiving end of an original gesture that takes time and special effort, something tailored to their passions and that makes them laugh. It will almost certainly be remembered for years to come.

Parents	Teachers

- Other fun gestures that can show our appreciation:
  - — arranging a special outing as a treat
  - — preparing her favorite meal
  - — having a sleepover with a friend
  - — buying a new cushion, lamp, or bedcover for her room

- Games and prizes work well as an end-of-term treat that recognizes the class's collective progress. Simple prizes of candy or chocolate or party bag gifts make it even more fun and special.

Hugs are for sharing

My teenage daughter got some wonderful SAT scores, and I hugged her to share her jubilation; but she clearly wanted it kept brief. I then turned to our dog, told him he was lucky to have such a clever mistress, and ruffled his head fondly. She laughed and immediately took him in her arms to receive, as it were, a second appreciative hug.

I like getting hugs. Not kissing you, though! That's yuck.

—Sarah, age 13

A hug is a physical gesture that enables us to share any feelings of joy or disappointment.

It is essentially nonjudgmental because it is empathic and it says, "I'm happy for you," as well as, "I am sad or happy or pleased with you." It is a two-way gesture, for the hug has to be accepted and reciprocated. When it finishes, it leaves our daughter holding the feeling, and there is nothing we can take away from her and use for our own benefit.

Some families don't feel comfortable with such physical closeness. They don't hug much or kiss or express themselves. As girls enter their teens, they may start to decline intimate parental embraces, particularly if they are dating. Passing on a hug to a pet dog or cat or to a soft toy that's an old favorite may help to convey an embrace without forcing one on her.

Parents	Teachers
• "Here's a hug [and make the gesture]. When you're ready for it, come and get it!"	• Teachers cannot hug children, but they are able to stand close or pat an arm or shoulder instead or express their delight in words.
• "Are you in the mood to share your happiness? How about my giving you a hug, then?"	
• "That's made me really happy. Give me a hug so I can share it with you."	

46 | Say it with surprises!

My mom bought a balloon with my name on it and put it in my bedroom for when I got home. I felt really special.

—Avni, age 10

Surprises are another way of saying thank you, or showing appreciation or love. A favorite meal; a plate of pieces of fruit arranged as a funny face, a spaceship, or a rocket; a surprise outing; a balloon that you have written or drawn on; an unexpected small present—all these are examples of surprises that can show appreciation of some special effort or simply say how much you have enjoyed your child that week or weekend.

Friday treats are a lovely way to sign off a school week. If a girl wants to know what the treat is "for," we can reply: to mark the end of a week's work or "because you are you!"

Parents	Teachers
• Treats and surprises don't have to be earned or deserved.	• Curriculum pressures often leave little space for surprises, but the end of the semester is a good moment to appreciate everyone's commitment and have fun together.
• If a treat is laden with hard-to-earn parental approval, it could make a child anxious and think, "But what if I'm not good or successful next time?"	
• The pleasure is the surprise and the thought, not the object itself. It can be really simple— and cheap!	
• "Today, just for fun, we're going on a mystery night walk with flashlights!"	

47 Let her feel whatever she feels

My six-year-old daughter's report card was very complimentary. Her teacher was especially positive about how well she was doing academically. When I said, "Good job," my daughter buried her face and choked, "It's a stupid report. What's the point of saying I'm good when it's so easy?"

Affirmation means we accept her as she is, not fashioned according to what we want to see because that makes life simpler. A girl who does well and thrives (for these are not the same things) is someone who knows herself and feels free to "be." If she feels able to feel sad, frustrated, happy, disappointed, angry, hateful, confident, frightened, or excited, she will probably experience her parents' tolerance and continuing presence and love throughout all these as a sign she can trust them and herself because they accept and trust all of her. She will feel understood, and if given the scope to decide when she will pull out all the stops, when she will coast, when she will explore her developing interests, and how she will use and allocate her time, she will be sufficiently confident to manage all of this sensibly.

Parents	Teachers
• Our feelings are the building blocks of ourselves.	• Acknowledge girls' feelings, but ensure that the rules about acceptable ways for them to be expressed are maintained.
• Allow your daughter to feel disappointed or angry if she doesn't do well—or if anything that you say is not well received.	
• If you take the time and trouble to understand the feelings that may explain her behavior, you will find out more about her.	
• It is normal for girls to feel angry, insulted, hostile, and proud, for girls are, like us, whole human beings. Ask yourself why her reactions bother you; don't put pressure on her to deny or ignore them.	

48 | Allow her to say it

It is not necessarily pigheaded or offensively arrogant for a child to believe she has done well and admit it. Indeed, high school students are increasingly encouraged to judge the quality of their own work as part of well-organized self-assessment programs. The successful Perry Pre-School Project, an educational research program, invited children as young as three to "plan, do, then review" the effectiveness of their chosen approaches to various tasks.

The possible downside of openly admitting to having been successful is pride and conceit. Children quickly identify "stuck-up" braggers and can turn against them ruthlessly; indeed, most children possess a deep-seated reticence about their talents and are not natural boasters. Perhaps those that do boast simply copy their parents! But the danger is avoided if we make clear that a girl's particular abilities do not make her better as a person than someone without those talents, and that she should never look down on anyone who performs differently. The knowledge that she's done her best and is doing well at whatever activity should stay private to her.

Parents	Teachers
• Teach that "good at" means "different from" not "better than" except at that particular skill.	• "I was very happy with this. Well done. Did you think you'd done it well?"
• Always ask, "Are you pleased with it?" or "Would you praise this?" and let her decide and say it.	• Encourage self-assessment, backed up with peer review and peer moderation.
• Girls tend to underestimate their work in self-assessment. If a girl says it's not good enough and she's not happy with it, ask what she thinks is wrong or weak and also what is good. She may then be encouraged to be less self-critical.	• Before you fill out report cards, ask students to anticipate your remarks. If there is a major discrepancy between your view and a student's, in either direction, discuss it with her later.

49 | Let siblings in on it

It should be part of living in a family that siblings value and appreciate each other's special achievements. Praise shouldn't always be issued from the top down. But this won't happen without everyone first having heard you say, "Well done" or "That's a lovely . . . ," simple phrases that are easy for all children to use. Whereas no child should have to take over a parent's responsibility for affirming or accepting a brother or sister, each child will feel more generous and open with praise and less threatened by or possessive of it when there is a genuine sharing of family appreciation and praise is not treated as a treasured winner's cup or an advantage to exploit.

Difficulties can arise when one sibling has talents or interests that enable her to be more enthusiastic and all-around successful than another. She may then attract more admiration from friends and family, creating an imbalance with her sibling. If this happens, ask the surrounding admirers to cool off; let the active sister learn to enjoy the pleasure she gains from her commitments and not seek other people's pleasure; and make sure that the other siblings receive plenty of loving attention and appreciation, which can often be more nourishing than accolades. Tensions, jealousies, and rivalries between siblings tend to appear either when one of them receives preferential attention so seems to be the favorite, or when the line between the achievement and the child becomes blurred.

Parents	Teachers

- Show joy in each of your children's varied milestones, pleasures, and personalities.

- Younger siblings can draw a picture as a gesture for their sister if she does well. Older ones can say, simply, "Well done," spend a little bit of time talking about the event, and come to watch the dance, play, match, or event a younger sister is involved with.

- Don't allow one child in particular to get all your acclaim and attention. If jealousy becomes destructively expressed, the balance you seek to achieve in your home will be upset.

- Positively value each child as an individual.

- Raise the suggestion that a sibling in the same school might like to know about some special outcome.

- Beware actually telling a brother or sister about a sibling's good efforts, in case your praise is misinterpreted as an underhanded incentive to improve.

50 | Watch out for *I*

Praise should focus more on the event or the child than on us. Once we start sentences with *I* the emphasis becomes our view of things. "I like the way . . . ," "I'm very pleased . . . ," "I think you could have done more to. . . . "I was so surprised you did so well . . . ," "I am convinced everything will go well for you because you have prepared so thoroughly." The earlier discussion of the purpose of praise highlighted such things as acknowledgment, attention, and affirmation. Children love to please their parents when they are young, but as they get older they need less parental pleasure and more affirmation and confirmation that they have judged things well and are on the right track, which will encourage confidence.

If a girl is hungry for praise, she will find any format rewarding, including all *I* phrases, but these won't help to wean her from any unhealthy reliance on our judgment. If she starts to sense she is being manipulated or too closely monitored, she may simply ignore all our comments. On the other hand, phrases such as "You did really well," "That was a brilliant result," or "The way you were able to reflect on that test paper and spot where you went wrong was impressive" are more focused on the process and are statements of fact that center on her, not of judgment that center on you.

Parents	Teachers

- "You are lovely as you are, *and* you're extra special to me!" is less loaded than "I love you as you are"—especially if she has just done something to please you.

- "You handled that really well; others might have lost their cool" is preferable to "I really liked the way you handled that."

- "You're such fun to be around" is less burdensome than "I love being around you when you're this cheerful."

- Free her: Focus your remarks on her ability to set about tasks well rather than offering your opinion on the outcome.

- "You've clearly got the measure of this problem now. This was a terrific assignment and shows what you are really capable of" is more convincing than "I am pleased you have understood this problem and done this piece of work so well."

Chapter 7

Common Mistakes to
Try to Avoid

Despite the best of intentions and our wish to help girls do well and show how much we love and appreciate them, we can still either say the wrong thing entirely or say the right thing at the wrong time or in the wrong way and, through clumsiness or ignorance, put our foot in it.

Though it may surprise some people, the worst offense is not necessarily criticism, some of which may be justified and valuable. It is not helpful to protect our child from every nuance of disapproval or disappointment. When she has misjudged or failed to understand things or ignored clear guidance, she should receive straightforward yet constructive, supportive explanations of what she can do differently next time. Constructive criticism is a far more helpful response than alternatives such as giving harsh punishment, using scathing sarcasm, turning a "blind eye," or even offering praise for effort if the outcome was way below expectation—and your daughter knows it. These can all have counterproductive consequences and are explored in this chapter.

The dangers that are associated with the wrong kind of attention, be it indiscriminate praise or constant criticism, include perfectionism (explored in Chapter 10), stress-inducing pressure, burnout and opting out, and, perhaps curiously, feelings of low self-worth. We might intend that our daughter feel pride and satisfaction, but this is not guaranteed. These outcomes, admittedly, lie at the extreme limits; signs of interim difficulty or more serious trouble ahead can include secretiveness, mild cheating and copying of other people's work, and learned helplessness.

The characteristic common to all the mistakes reviewed here is placing our concerns and desires before our daughter's feelings and wishes: a failure to treat her as an autonomous human being. Each child should, then, be allowed to be who she is and not be compared to anyone else or used by us as a vehicle to make good any missed opportunities of our own that we may now regret. She should be given the freedom to say no or stop and be offered every opportunity to do well for her own pleasure, not simply to please us. Parents often need to step in temporarily to help a girl over a sticky patch—for example, not understanding some math or getting disenchanted with her progress on a musical instrument and wanting to give up—but when she has overcome the problem, we should withdraw, allowing her from then on to set her own pace and direction.

51 | Think about why you're offering praise

When we consider whether to give what we may see as the "gift" of praise, we look first at what our child has done and whether the behavior or circumstance warrants it. Our focus is therefore on her and is context-bound and time-limited: The conscious part of our attention is fixed on her. But less obvious ulterior motives often lurk behind our apparently altruistic actions or comments that have more to do with us—our dreams, desires, and fears—than with her. We applaud certain attributes to help her achieve aims we consider desirable. We can so easily try to turn her into what we want her to be.

At one level, this is inevitable. Of course it is a parent's job to encourage socially acceptable behavior and discourage actions that will set her back or get her into trouble. We do shape children's behavior and should do so, as gardeners prune growing plants so they develop stronger stems and larger flowers. But we should be careful not to take a cutting from ourselves and graft it onto them or to cut and style so much that they need walls or wires to shore them up. We should not contrive to bolster our own vulnerable self-worth with our daughter's success, but instead to give her the autonomy she needs even if this means she does not choose the future we dream for her.

Parents	Teachers

- Consider if you are making a point of being positive to compensate for being very preoccupied recently, or if you could be saying the "right things" to make your daughter feel more loving toward you because you need more support.

- If the answer to either of these is yes or possibly, beware of your motives and manipulation. Better to address the issue directly or at its source.

- Watch carefully how she responds to the different ways in which you express approval and delight.

- As much as you can, turn the attention back to her: "Yes, I do like it, but the more important thing is whether you do"; "To me, you did very well, but were you pleased with the result?"

- If praise is natural, it will roll off the tongue without much forethought.

- Individual girls who have a despondent personality may need more encouragement than others.

52 | Ban the word *good*; it does girls no good

Good is such a bad word when it comes to ensuring that praise is effective. It is bad because it is inadequate, for it says so little. It is a shorthand word used to convey many things and sometimes some not very helpful things. It is also bad because it automatically conjures up the idea of the opposite, which is *bad,* and if a girl is not told she is good, the inference is that she is, or could be, bad when she is not being good. *Good* and *bad* are not just black-and-white words but black *or* white words. When a "good" girl is being less obliging or is just behaving normally, she will often be called "bad," which is neither fair nor beneficial to her learning. Girls may decide that striving to be good in order to please is the best strategy for them because it is the safest. But this may make a girl unwilling to push the envelope, take risks, explore untried skills, or examine who she really is.

One use of the word *good* is "Good, you did what I wanted you to do, and you behaved in the way I hoped you would." A good child may therefore tend to be passive: She is not noisy, boisterous, messy, curious, or clumsy and does not break things. She is that particular parent's perfect child. And that's the point. Girls who are required to be good and are rewarded amply for being so can lose their sense of individuality and identity as they fill the mold shaped by their parents' expectations. They become clones and clams—the silent types—to avoid the danger of disapproval.

Parents	Teachers

Parents

- Instead of *good,* we can say *clever, organized, thoughtful, helpful,* or *creative* or just say, "You're a happy girl." If she has done something she's pleased with, that's what she'll be feeling.

- Instead of labeling her *bad* or *naughty,* we should turn it around to our view: "I found that rather selfish," "I didn't like that behavior."

- To convey our delight in her, we can say, "You're my lovable girl!" the prerequisite for positive self-esteem.

Teachers

- "Very good" on a piece of work tells the student very little about what she did right, and she may not be sure of this. Instead, you could write, "Very well argued," "Very well remembered," "Very good use of detail," "Lovely description—I saw it all!"

- "Good" girls should be not so good to teach. Really impressive students will inevitably question and challenge academically as well as deliver.

53 Don't turn your dream into her success—or nightmare

I told her, I don't care if you fell and smashed your nose. Your ice skating is your job and you've just got to get up again and get on with it.

—Mother of a 9-year-old ice-skating starlet
when her daughter fell during practice
(The mother had also skated competitively as a
child but had given up before reaching the top.)

Being successful does not necessarily generate psychological health and confidence, as we see in the tips on perfectionism. Where girls are required to carry and make a reality of their parents' dreams, they are not usually free to take things in a direction or at a pace that suits them, mix and match their free-time activities to create a better balance, or decide when they have had enough. For success to create confidence and security rather than anxiety and insecurity, girls must believe they are following their own wishes. Mothers and fathers must beware that gymnastics or ice dancing really is just for fun, and not to make up for their near miss in the competitive stakes. Or, they should be clear, for example, that tennis coaching helps their daughter to explore, exploit, and enjoy the sport, rather than to fulfill a parent's dream or, worse, to generate generous prize money for their personal long-term financial gain.

Parents	Teachers

- Girls are not puppets—they are growing people.

- "Who is she doing it for—for her or for me?" is a very important question that should be asked at every stage of a girl's progress if she is performing competitively. And answer it honestly.

- Don't compete with, criticize, or ridicule her. Every challenge drags her into your territory and reinforces her belief that your view and preferences must be better.

- Give her room to be herself. It's your problem, not hers, if you feel uncomfortable with her preferred interests and direction.

- Vary your teaching style and lessons. Your comfort zones, passions, and communication methods may not suit all the girls in your class.

- Encourage tolerance and mutual respect of the differences between all students so they learn not to impose their values and choices on others.

54 | Don't take the credit for her success

Sometimes parents invest so much of their time and effort in helping their daughter to achieve the hoped-for success that they are convinced it could never have been achieved without them. They may have spent hours coaching her or sacrificed a great deal to pay for a private tutor. They may have imposed strict practice regimes or been genuinely supportive when something went awry so that a child was able to find her own way back to confidence through tolerance. These circumstances enable parents to take responsibility for the success, expressed either privately or openly, which can then undermine their daughter's contribution. Offering rewards and incentives can have the same effect, making parental intervention the critical factor. When parents steal some of the credit, which is what this amounts to, a child may feel empty and used simply as a tool to generate a parent's self-esteem.

Comments such as "I told you that you were a 'natural,' that's why I signed you up for the course" or "Congratulations for making the team. Aren't you pleased now that I put you on that healthier diet?" clearly claim some of the credit.

Parents	Teachers

- Pass your possible part over to your daughter: "You became so much more organized. Nice job"; "When you started to look after yourself and care about your health it really paid off"; "You took real advantage of the extra experience that course gave you"; "You've developed a lovely relationship with books and it probably helped."

- If your friend's daughter does particularly well at something, it is more appropriate to focus on the girl's pleasure than to attribute any of the success to your friend and congratulate her. Instead, say: "I hear Juanita did really well; she must be delighted."

- Credit the class or individual, not yourself. If you helped, that is no more than your professional duty.

- "I was just the fertilizer— you put down the roots and did the growing!"

55 "I'm so proud of you!"

Which of the following would you be most likely to say? "I'm really proud of you for managing that!" "I hope you feel proud of yourself for doing that—you deserved to do well after all that effort." "You probably feel really proud to have achieved that." "I feel so proud of you and proud to have you as my child."

A group of teenagers agreed that the parental phrase they most loved to hate was "I'm so proud of you." They found it hard to explain why this response grated so much, but the problem seemed to relate to its being "over the top" as well as causing discomfort because a parent was too emotionally involved in their work. They did not want the responsibility for delivering or maintaining their parent's sense of pride, and they certainly had not worked hard for a particular test or exam so their parent could feel that way—they had done it for themselves and for their own reasons.

Our role should be to enable our daughter to feel proud, independently and regardless of our feelings, because she knows what she set out to achieve and how much effort she needed to apply.

Parents	Teachers

Parents

- Keep comments as free from judgment as possible. "You probably felt really proud when you heard that" implies that if she did feel that, you can understand why. If not, no matter.

- Even, "I hope you feel proud of that result" implies that if she doesn't, she should because your view counts.

- Pride can be an unjustified opinion: Be careful you're not exaggerating her achievement.

- Pride might, indeed, come before a fall if, as a result of your insistence that she excel in one activity, she decides to avoid the pressure and drop it.

Teachers

- You can be proud of the achievement of a class—proud of everyone or of your professional input—but your pride is of no relevance to any individual's success.

- "I am really impressed by your progress," "You deserve to feel proud of your achievement," or "I'm so pleased you have understood things and can now work closer to your true ability level" are more appropriate remarks for individual students.

Keep it clean: no sarcasm or caveats

Ninety-nine percent. That's not bad! But why did you let one get away?
> —The comment of a mother to
> her 16-year-old daughter

When adults are uncomfortable with giving praise, they often lace it with something rather nasty—a sting or kickback—to qualify and downgrade the compliment and make it not quite the generous gesture it might have been. This is a sufficiently common practice so that it has been given a name: *contaminative praise*. It can become a style or habit, is sometimes dressed up as humor, and is not always said to hurt; yet it usually does. The child is not quite let off the hook and still needs to wait for the full approval that frees her to move on.

Contaminative praise is probably uncomfortably familiar. Examples of such comments include "This report card is great, but why did you have to take so long to mend your ways?" "That model is really lovely—no one would know you used to be all fingers and thumbs!" "Your bedroom looks so much tidier now; terrific, but it won't stay this way long—you'll see!"

Parents	Teachers

- Imagine praise as a cookie: Would you give your daughter a cookie as a reward, then, just as she reaches for it, pull it back, shake salt onto it, and then return it for her to eat? No? So why would you effectively do that with praise?

- Sarcasm is said to be the lowest form of wit.

- If you see it as harmless fun, reflect on the essence of humor. Is making jokes at other people's expense— especially the expense of children, who won't see it the same way—the only way to have fun and make others laugh?

- Sarcasm is neither an effective nor a professional tool for teachers. It should never be used as it confuses and humiliates.

57 Absence makes children's hearts grow harder

My two-year-old daughter was looked after during the day by a neighbor's daughter for two months when I took a short-term job. This babysitter was warm and wonderful, devising many great things to do. But then she went off to college. She turned on the charm and enthusiasm very naturally on her first return visit, and my daughter loved it. But after each absence my daughter became increasingly confused and then actually turned away and refused to engage.

For adults, so the saying goes, absence makes the heart grow fonder. This is not the case for children, who find unexpected or longer absences due to work trips or hospitalization much harder to understand and endure because they need to trust and rely on people for their security. Young children in particular are likely to feel at least a little bit abandoned, unwanted, or at fault when, for example, they start day care and it is unfamiliar; largely because they are extremely egocentric, they often believe the absence must be a punishment for wrongdoing: The very young frequently make sense of information and experience in unexpected ways.

We sometimes cover our guilt for periods of absence by being extra attentive, fawning and overrewarding our children when we return. This may console and convince a younger girl for a while but then could confuse and bother her so that she stops trusting the praise.

Parents	Teachers

- If you have to be away frequently, develop clear and predictable routines and rituals that mark your leavings and your returns so your daughter can learn to predict and trust your love despite your absence.

- Try not to be overexuberant when you come home, especially if you expect to be away again soon or to be very preoccupied, which can amount to the same thing. A calm, close, intimate, tight cuddle may be more effective than bellows of delight with multiple presents showered on her.

- If you have had to take time off from the classroom at unpredictable moments, don't expect your encouraging feedback to have quite the same positive impact when you return. It takes time to rebuild the trust.

- Girls who have felt rejected and constantly criticized or manipulated by their parents may reject any form of appreciation or approval from their teachers because they will find it hard to accept it as truth.

- For a disbelieving student, select one thing only to comment on positively, and mention it six times every day. Eventually, she will begin to see herself differently and accept that she is worthy of appreciation.

Accentuate the positive— but notice the negative

When you're upset about something that hasn't gone well, I'd prefer they tell you what they really think, instead of saying it was fine and it doesn't matter.

—Emma, age 11

I prefer to hear, "At least you tried hard, even if you didn't do so well," rather than "That was good," which wouldn't be true.

—Alex, age 15

It is fine to accentuate the positive, especially when girls are young and often cannot help being clumsy or overexuberant, but as they get older the negative should increasingly be noticed, not ignored. A young girl will make lots of mistakes either of judgment or about her physical competence; it is hard for her to think ahead, rules are hard to grasp, and she will get tired and fractious or need attention. We should understand and tolerate these errors that cannot really be considered "naughty," and we should certainly not punish her. At a period of life when mistakes and accidents abound, she should be allowed to start her life feeling positive, capable, and confident, not cowed by constant criticism and failure.

But by the time girls reach the age of six or seven, the negatives should be noted and addressed. "Accentuate the positive" means, essentially, to emphasize helpful behavior and to make it conspicuous, but that does not mean we should ignore outrageous behavior or go overboard with overdone exaggerations when the event is modest.

Parents	Teachers

- "I love going with you to the store, but this time it was not fun. It's not okay for you to go on and on about having something to eat or to nag about missing your TV show. You're usually great company, but I'll think about going alone if it happens again."

- "It clearly matters to you that you came in fifth today. Was there a special reason you wanted to do better?" is preferable to "But darling, you did just great, so don't get so upset!"

- Be straightforward but constructive, too. Focus any comments on ways to improve on the next piece of work rather than highlight the shortcomings of the work under scrutiny. This approach leaves children feeling okay.

59 | Don't compare her to others

When our girls are babies, it is natural for all of us to look for similarities between our brand-new infant and our partner, her siblings, and other relatives so that everyone feels she is part of the family immediately. Not long after, however, the comparisons with others can become far less benign.

Comments like these can be upsetting: "Your brother would not have dreamed of behaving like that," "Why can't you be an A student like your sister?" or "Carrie eats everything when she comes here—why are you so picky?" Those who lived with such taunts say that, far from being a spur to action, their childhood was tainted by them.

Even handing out equal praise or favorable comparisons can be a hindrance. Saying, "Jerry's the brain box and Maria's the family athlete" may give each child something to be proud of but limits the likelihood that either will explore their full talent in the other's special sphere. And comparisons with parents of the "You take after me" variety can be dangerous, too. You may have been a budding musician and played in local concerts at the same age your daughter is performing, but let her achievement be unsullied by inheritance. Any girl will want to be herself and not likened to anyone else.

Parents	Teachers

- Each child will respond in her own individual way to a situation because she is unique. Comparisons may stunt her development and undermine her confidence in herself.

- Make it clear that there is room for more than one mathematician, poet, pianist, or tennis star in the family.

- Don't compare your daughter with how you were or what you did at her age. She is herself, not you, and you've probably glamorized the memory!

- Labeling makes children resentful and can tempt them to do the opposite out of spite.

- See each child as an individual, not in the context of her family. Never compare her to a sibling to disparage, coerce, or even praise her work.

- The most useful, and constructive, comparison to make is with her previous best work or performance.

- Be especially supportive of originality and creativity, through which she is exploring and expressing her difference.

60 | Don't swamp her with your success

Acorns seldom grow under the great oak.

If we want our daughter to be able gradually to recognize when she's done well and be open about her pleasure in her accomplishments rather than rely on us for warm words, we can set an example by describing occasions when things go well for us. However, it is possible for parents to go too far and swamp their daughter with their success and thus overemphasize its value. It is important to leave room for her to feel that small advances are worthwhile and valuable, and to avoid implying that each child has to excel to fit in—or suffer derision or rejection.

Where parental success is paraded, it can create an impossible act to follow. Though many daughters follow in their father's or mother's footsteps and are happy to do so, legions of others get put off by the anticipated competition and feel intimidated by any expectation to match their parents' achievement. The best gauge of balance in the matter is whether we suggest we are better as a person for our success and feel superior, which is dangerous. If, on the other hand, we explain it as the result of hard work, luck, and embracing opportunity, we are less likely to arouse complex reactions, resentments, and fears.

Parents	Teachers

- Handle your own successes with sensitivity. Convey surprise rather than worthiness, and attribute it to your judgment, hard work, and good fortune, not genius.

- Any significant success of yours will be evident; there'll be no need to blow your own horn.

- Don't strive to excel at everything. Doing something well enough, and sometimes not quite making it, sets a healthier example.

- Where two parents are successful in different fields, a girl may find it harder to find her own niche. So value her particular strengths, and don't compete with one another, either!

- When a girl struggles with a problem of understanding, you won't help her by declaring that it is really very simple and then reexplaining it in the same way and at the same speed.

- Ask if anyone in the class is willing to describe how she made sense of the task or procedure.

- Underachieving girls will be motivated by the successful efforts of other strugglers, not by the success of the class star.

Chapter 8

Bribes, Rewards, and Incentives

The tactic so many parents resort to in order to nudge their reluctant daughter into action is offering bribes. That's what most people call them, but they are more correctly described as inducements, in the form of incentives and rewards. A bribe is something offered to persuade someone to do something illegal or wrong, whereas what we generally offer is an incentive to persuade our child to undertake something legal and desirable—and, usually, in her own interest—that otherwise she would not do. Perhaps we use the term *bribe* because we feel some guilt about what we're doing as it is seen as a last resort and we would prefer that it was not necessary.

Incentives and rewards can work well, but with girls, they must be used very carefully, at all ages. When girls are very young, although tactics such as star charts and stickers can help impatient and lively youngsters with short time horizons see their progress represented visually and help impulsive children to control their strong desires, the approach can reinforce and internalize the importance of being "good." On top of this, an additional danger is that even five-year-olds can get fresh and argue about whether a particular target has or has not been reached. They can debate how many stars any special success or behavior deserves, so an approach designed to end battles that seemed simple can itself create friction if handled with too much flexibility and without appreciating the extent to which a girl will try to take some control if she feels manipulated. For example, it can be foolhardy to offer girls special rewards for eating if there are concerns, for this may introduce a further level of interference that could have sparked the problem initially.

The truth is that parents often use incentives to engineer a particular outcome they consider desirable. Presenting suggestions and goals in this way may multiply the opportunities to please, but if they are overused, girls can feel entangled by the rewards and affronted that they are not trusted, a reaction that may reawaken any dormant self-doubt.

Boys tend to play power games with rewards and argue the merits or refuse to cooperate. Girls are subtle, more manipulative, and more inclined to use emotional blackmail. They may curry favor close to results time to get a bigger reward; they may pester for a reward when the parent has not considered one; they may whine that so-and-so has received some treat and imply that you are being mean. If this script sounds familiar, it's time to prepare your defenses and reconsider your tactics.

There is no obvious age after which rewards and incentives are best avoided. What's a more relevant issue is each child's personality and maturity, the problem at hand, and how successfully rewards have been deployed in the past. However, the closer children are to college and working life, the more they need to rely on motivating themselves.

61 | Be clear about the purpose

Incentives come in various forms and send various messages. There is the "sweeten the pill" incentive, which we use to show we realize that something is difficult. We might say, "I can see that you might run out of steam because this is quite a challenge. When you're through, I'll give you something to show I appreciate what you've done."

There is the "kick in the rear" incentive that says, in effect, "I'm not sure you'll do it without something to tempt you." For example, you might offer her a hundred dollars if she manages to reach the age of sixteen without smoking.

There is also the negative or threatening incentive. Instead of offering some prize, the inducement is to avoid experiencing an outright penalty or even simply not receiving something they otherwise would have. A parent might say, "Unless you improve your grade average, I won't pay for your driving lessons as I did your brother's" or "If you don't quit teasing your sister, I'll take away all your Barbies."

Parents	Teachers

- Think carefully about whether your reasons for offering an incentive are justified or if there is an alternative approach that may be more suitable, such as showing interest in a project and offering to hear a daily progress report.

- Consider the importance of the particular target or outcome in question. If it marks a crucial turning point or if something very significant hangs on it, there may be more reason to encourage her to do her very best.

- Ask whether your daughter wants or needs a reward or incentive. She could now be old enough to appreciate the importance of this moment, too, and she may want to meet the challenge without help.

- Think whether any incentive you offer will help a girl to do her best, or whether it is meant to raise your overall results.

62 | Rewards are more effective as surprises

I prefer surprises. It's nice when they've put time and effort into something.

—Stephanie, age 11

A reward can be agreed on in advance as an incentive, or it can be offered afterward, produced as a surprise in recognition of our appreciation. Rewards are most helpful and enjoyable if they are not announced in advance, for two reasons. Given in this way, they not only prevent any unpleasant negotiation about whether the suggested reward is big enough but also reduce the chance that any girl will intentionally underperform in order to continue to benefit.

My grandmother, brought up over a century ago, used to warn all of us grandchildren, "I want doesn't get." It was a typical Edwardian homily, designed to warn children against covetousness. Surprises aren't dangled beforehand and are therefore more spontaneous and far less open to manipulation by either side.

Parents	Teachers

Parents

- Keep any reward as a genuine surprise. A financial reward that is pried out of you afterward is not a surprise. Praise is a form of reward. We generally reject the practice of double punishment, so why should we be so open to double rewards?

- In order to make our gesture a surprise, it follows that we cannot produce rewards too often.

- Surprises do not have to cost money. But the more toys and goodies children possess, the harder it can be to find simple ways to please them. Examples could include cooking together, letting her use something of yours that she covets, or staying up later one weekend.

Teachers

- Giving surprises to individual students could lay a teacher open to the charge of favoritism. However, activities that students enjoy, such as having extra time on the computer, can be offered as a surprise reward.

- Beware rewarding girls who seek to become teacher's pets by acting the goody-goody.

63 | Keep targets manageable: Ask whether she can realistically deliver

Girls like to work with adults who have confidence in them and ask them to stretch, because that is when they give their best and make progress. Doing well when the challenge is easy is neither exciting nor rewarding. But challenges must be set to tempt children to develop themselves, not put them off because they are overambitious and feel threatening. A target set too high is as unhelpful as one set too low.

We know that a target or expectation is realistic when the girl involved agrees that it is achievable. If her view is more pessimistic than ours, she may reject the objective and the reward before she starts. We should never set up our child to fail. If goals appear to her consistently unrealistic, the reward will never be earned, and the result may be either a disenchanted and more self-doubting child who refuses to engage at all, or a heated argument about how close she got and what other recognition she might deserve, given the advance she did achieve.

Parents	Teachers
• Ask your daughter what she thinks she can handle.	• Make sure the goal, deadline, and expectations are clear.
• Help her to devise clear plans to meet her goal.	• Help girls to assess whether the conditions have been met, and face the consequences if not.
• If she seeks an easier target, start there and work up. Self-belief is so important to longer-term striving it must be securely in place.	• If you detect underconfidence, suggest that a girl prepare a detailed study plan so she realizes that the goal is possible.
• Girls often underestimate their ability and do not usually aim low simply to get an easier ride. If your daughter is pessimistic, it could signify a fragile confidence that needs attention.	• Don't constantly move the goalposts, as this may suggest that her achievement was somehow not good enough. Ask whether she's ready for the next challenge or needs some time for everything to settle.
• Encourage her to mix short and longer-term goals.	

**Reward her with
your presence, not presents**

*Grandma always comes with little gifts for us, but I
still prefer Grandpa because he takes the time to
talk to us, and he seems nicer and kinder.*

—Julia, age 7

Rewards are used, typically, as a sign that we appreciate
what our daughter did and to encourage her. Another
good reason for using rewards, when they are used with
care, is that they give children little boosts along the
otherwise endless journey that is growing and learning.

Children seem naturally materialistic. Any girl will
catch on very quickly to how much things cost and
will be hawkish as she watches and assesses whether a
sibling or, especially, a stepsibling gets better gifts than
she does. But girls are also hardwired to detect insincer-
ity or superficial gestures, as indicated in the quote
above. They know how easy it is for many—though not
all—parents to buy something. The best way to show
that we truly appreciate a daughter's effort is to put
some effort into our gesture, which means sharing our
scarcest resource: time. As one ten-year-old said, "I'm
one of five, so one-to-one time with my mom or dad is
special." Our time with her will genuinely encourage
her; will demonstrate genuine appreciation, regard, and
approval; and has infinite, not specific, value.

Parents	Teachers
• Depending on her age, watch your daughter doing something she enjoys, sit with her while she eats, chat as she falls asleep, give her a ride to friends', or play a game.	• Find a moment to have a special quiet conversation that details a student's achievement and shows you are interested in and value her as an individual.
• Quiet time together can be as important as action-packed time. Turn your phone off!	• Demonstrate personal attention by relating the current work to something she wrote previously.
• Give more generously of your time if there have been any problems or family difficulties recently, as she may be unsettled and will almost certainly need you more.	• Point out what this good piece of work means for her future possibilities and potential.

65 | Let her help to choose the treat or incentive

I don't get presents. I prefer something I've wanted to do, like an outing or trip to the movies.

—Rena, age 10

This will lessen the possibility that she may see the incentive as a surreptitious attempt by us to control her as it is a celebration on her terms.

If we choose the treat, we have to guess what she would like, and we might get it wrong—missing something either obvious or an as-yet-undisclosed passion. If she helps to choose the treat, it can still be a nice surprise. After a pleasing outcome, we can say she deserves a treat, and she can help to select it; we must not forget to give some guidance as to the appropriate scale or cost of the gift or event.

During the treat, she can feel like a queen, having special influence and attention for a short while, as on a birthday, which will contrast strongly with her daily diet of school, where she has to fall into line, be one of a very large crowd, and sometimes play second fiddle to friends.

Parents	Teachers
• The choice of treat will necessarily vary according to a girl's age. It could be a little toy, some candy, an extra story at bedtime, something that relates to her personal passion or hobby, choosing the destination for a special trip out, a DVD to watch just with you or with the whole family on the weekend, or the choice of menu for a celebratory meal at home or out.	• There is less room for choice in a classroom context, but rather than determine what the treat should be, offer one or two choices if this is feasible.

66 Money talks—back, so take care if you use it!

My brother always asks for something ahead of time, and his list is so long!

—Paula, age 8

Children often argue about the size of the reward they deserve and push for more. What was intended as a generous gesture can degenerate into a battle of wits and power. "I'll do it for ten dollars, not for only five" is a not unfamiliar cry in households where money talks loudly and is used to ensure that parental will prevails. Even small children can barter over the appropriate payment for, for example, being good at the dentist.

To negotiate every nickel is an obvious way to take control in a situation in which a girl senses financial manipulation. And if money is always accorded value as a reward, it may also become something she desires strongly—and takes—if she ever feels ignored and resentful.

Adolescent girls may be especially prone to con and wheedle their dads. If they associate femininity with flirting and see dads or boys as potential soft touches and game for a challenge, which many girls do, they're more likely to try their dads than their moms, who know the game and will play it back straight.

Parents	Teachers

Parents

- If you hear, "My friends have all been given a hundred dollars for doing well," don't automatically cough it up. Her real reward is discovering later that life's best rewards are rarely financial.

- Lack of money may be a convenient temporary excuse. But if you've made it a habit to give money as a reward, when any appears she'll be there, hand held out.

- We might give something freely, but the recipients often ask why.

- Where money talks, it implies that spending is best, that money buys influence, and that money matters more than time.

Teachers

- Ask for students' views about the value of money as a reward in class discussion time.

- Point out that the more money children receive via financial rewards, the less they need; unless the amount rises, the incentive becomes progressively devalued.

- Reflect on how much you value your job because of or despite the money you receive.

67 Don't let money become the family's emotional currency

Mom and I had a huge falling out yesterday. She felt so guilty about it that she took me out today and bought me a load of new clothes.

—Carrie, age 17

No girl should ever feel the bigger the present or the more money she is given, the more she is loved. Love cannot and should not be measured by price tags. How much you love a child should never become linked to how much money you are prepared to spend on her. When effort, commitment, and love become closely equated with money and costly gifts, children can ask for ever bigger gifts for proof of love and use emotional blackmail to get them.

Blackmail may occur when gifts are used to fill emotional or time gaps in relationships, and when they are purchased either to say sorry or to assuage guilt. Of course all dads and moms like to buy a little gift after a trip away, but if it stops being a surprise and becomes an expectation, we have to take stock. Any complaint along the lines that something more was expected because the trip was a long one will show it is time to think afresh about how we make up for any time she misses us.

Parents	Teachers
• When financial rewards become emotional currency, children can think, "Prove you're really pleased by giving more," or "I did it anyway, but heck, let's lay on some guilt and see what happens!"	• When girls are used to relationships at home that are conditional and based on trading, they may try the same tactics with you. Understand where this might come from, and be quiet and firm rather than angry.
• Stand up for yourself: Don't let your daughter exploit your love; ensure she knows, through the little things that you do and say, that you love her without proving it by giving presents.	• Remember the theory: The key to safe striving is to ensure that motivation is self-generated, not created by someone else either playing on guilt or applying undue pressure.
• If you feel guilty about frequent absence, talk to her directly about how sad this makes you and call her as regularly as you can at an agreed-on time so she knows she is "kept in mind." Presents will then be less necessary.	

> *Where motivation rests upon extrinsic guilt or pres-*
> *sure, there is less sense of self-determination.*
> —Howard Hall, professor of
> sport and exercise psychology

Psychological theory distinguishes between "intrinsic" and "extrinsic" rewards. Extrinsic rewards are those that exist outside the child, for example, money, toys, new clothes, or perhaps the present of a pet. *The Concise Oxford Dictionary* defines *extrinsic* as "not belonging to, not essential."

Internal, or intrinsic, rewards, by contrast, belong naturally. They lie inside each of us as positive thoughts and experiences and can be understood as essential. Examples of internal rewards are pride and pleasure; a satisfied curiosity; a sense of mastery and capability; or feeling fit, healthy, and agile. Rewards are usually offered as encouragement to increase motivation, yet we know the most effective motivation is self-motivation. We all have to learn to do things because we want to, and because we enjoy the satisfaction that usually flows from effort, progress, and achievement. Girls need to learn to acknowledge and value these feelings and consider them sufficient reward.

Parents	Teachers

- When something goes well, ask your daughter how she feels so she learns to "read" and acknowledge the internal benefits of making an effort and doing herself justice.

- External rewards depend on others; they pale as they become predictable and eventually become mere tokens of success. To remain an effective incentive, they have to increase.

- Internal rewards, by contrast, are within each person's control. If the pleasure of success fades, she simply raises the target.

- Try to ensure that each girl understands and feels comfortable inside with the grade given or comment made and that she has learned something.

- Make sure the benefit is doing well, not simply receiving the accolade or bonus points. The older girls get, the more they like to gamble with manipulative games with rewards, and they may get hooked.

69 If rewards backfire, drop them

Rewards and incentives may backfire for several reasons. A girl may refuse to accept them, she may argue endlessly about the nature of the reward, or she may go so far but stop just short of the agreed-on threshold and still demand the reward. If any tactic is no longer working or has turned sour, how should we respond?

The first action is to stop using rewards altogether, rather than try to devise another that may work better. The next is to reflect on why this strategy has become a problem. It could be that she wants to show that she doesn't need them. She might be rebelling against being treated like a puppet and wants more autonomy in her life. It may be that her self-confidence has taken a tumble for some reason, so she is now frightened of failing and is no longer trying. It is also quite possible that she has simply got too big for her britches and is pushing her luck.

Parents	Teachers
• Indicate you are pleased to drop the use of rewards because you prefer to rely on trust.	• Rewards systems have to be consistent throughout any school. If the system does not seem to work with individual students, think more deeply about the possible explanation. Consider the experience of colleagues and brainstorm potentially more effective and flexible approaches, such as making specific tasks easier (fewer spellings to learn) or providing a quiet place to do homework in school with you or a colleague present to help the girl concentrate.
• Convey clearly that you are confident your daughter can and will deliver, for her own benefit and future.	
• If you need to, remind her, firmly, of any agreement, and restate that you assume it will be adhered to.	
• Once she reaches the age of about ten, invite her to summarize the arguments in favor of working and trying hard and the downside of letting things slip. Avoid hectoring her and talking at her.	

> *The competitive instinct can lead to shallow growth and the Brownie badge collecting mentality.*
> —Tony Gardiner, professor of mathematics

Girls compete in different ways and over different things. For example, they attach a great deal of importance to how they look and believe that having fashionable clothes and a slim figure as well as brains will help to make them popular—the ultimate prize.

Research shows that when either parents or teachers set up competitions to raise performance, the outcome is often an anxious child. If a child feels that something important hangs on a test result, she is more likely either to experience pretest nerves and debilitating panic or to become depressed if there is a disappointing result. The more parents encourage competition and demand top results, the more a girl could be tempted to cheat or impede others to secure the advantage and approval.

Parents	Teachers
• Make sure your daughter has a right to be heard and the chance to be understood.	• Make sure every girl has a right to be heard and the chance to be understood.
• Encourage active and appropriate participation and involvement at all times.	• It is through having responsibility that children find out about themselves. Put girls in charge of as much of their own learning and assessment as possible, and give them jobs around the class or school where possible.
• She will make the effort when she knows she can say her piece and will be respected.	

Chapter 9

Using Praise to Encourage Learning and Behavior

It would not be surprising if many readers turned to this chapter first. People often seek guidance when they feel things are going off the track. In terms of what is a common problem to parents, school performance and behavior are the two big ones. Praise, encouragement, and positive feedback are especially valuable and effective in these two areas and are far more likely to produce happier and more self-directed children than punishment, harsh criticism, or humiliation. These are also the areas in which parents can find themselves in trouble, despite using a range of "positive" and recommended inducements, without really understanding why. That's why it's important for parents to know the general principles of effective praise (and some of the pitfalls of effusive praise) before they seek answers to any immediate problem. It is also important to be clear about the best ways to get the best from our children.

But first, a few words about learning and discipline. The better these are understood, the easier it will be to keep feedback positive and constructive.

Learning is an emotional activity and a very complex process. It involves far more than a child's simply opening her mind and receiving knowledge because her *state* of mind—how she feels and interprets the world around her—inevitably influences her willingness and capacity to absorb information. When children struggle at school, there are frequently complex explanations. Difficult life events, including teasing, can distress and preoccupy children so they're unable to concentrate. These same events may threaten children's self-belief because they often introduce uncertainty and powerlessness, making children less willing to take the risks that learning entails. Learning can also arouse a range of fears: fear of incompetence, fear of failure, fear of reprimand, and fear of ridicule. Ultimately, children are agents of their own learning. Rather than be forced to absorb information and then receive the "gift" of positive feedback, it is better that a girl be offered the chance to decide and say *how* best she learns, *when* she is ready to try harder, or *whether* she needs tokens of appreciation.

Discipline should also encourage self-discipline and autonomy. Girls should not be forced to comply with adult rules and wishes in every sphere of their lives. Challenging behavior should be understood more than punished. Early on, of course, it is important to set your daughter clear guidelines to keep her safe and secure, but as she grows older she should be encouraged to make choices, judge situations for herself, and assess both the consequences of and her reasons for making particular choices. Eventually, by her late teens, she should develop her own priorities and values. Parents and teachers will encourage this self-discipline if they value and reward girls' reflection and responsibility and treat compliance more as an expectation.

I had a greater sense of achievement from finishing 73rd in the national school championships aged fourteen than from coming sixth in the 10,000 meters in the 1972 Olympics which I was expected to win. It was a disaster for me. But I tried to hang on to the positive view that I was sixth best in the world.

—David Bedford, British athlete who created the annual London Marathon

It is important to realize that what might be a small, unremarkable step forward for one girl can be a significant mark of progress for another, and a successful result for someone who needs to work hard to do well may be a disappointing one for someone else who rides challenges easily and is capable of better. No one should be denied her parents' pleasure just because someone with greater talent was in the lineup to outshine her personal effort.

In school, children are viewed as learners and are judged and differentiated by academic ability. At home, we must see our daughter in the round and as multitalented, always offer a sense of hope, and help her develop the self-respect necessary to acquire a positive self-image even if academic excellence is not her strong point.

Parents	Teachers

- Every girl learns and develops in a different way and takes a different amount of time. "She's a late developer" may be the truth, rather than a convenient, embarrassed cover-up response to skeptical friends or relatives.

- Remember that stressful experiences can put learning on hold. And everyone needs times when she treads water rather than surges forward.

- Ask your daughter whether it felt good to her. If it did and she's not pretending, that's good enough.

- If your friends' children are doing "better" than yours, avoid feeling competitive. Yours are still loveable as they are.

- Consider each piece of work as a good or less good one *for each student at this moment,* not in relation to the standard you ultimately expect.

- Whole-class praise is good from time to time so everyone feels the benefit.

72 | Match the applause to the achievement

Oh, good job, Sunita! I love how you are sitting quietly at the table! Everyone, put your hands together for a little clap!

"Say it enthusiastically" is a mantra adopted by many parenting and management gurus and therefore by parents. Of course, it is undoubtedly better to sound pleased than to describe pleasure with a deadpan expression and a flat voice; however, the fervor espoused by many can go too far in the other direction and not only sound fake but also create too much tension around the requirement to continue to deserve the accolades.

If praise is about appreciation, and appreciation involves estimating the worth of something, we need to match the applause to the achievement.

Parents	Teachers
• Encouragement includes waiting quietly and patiently while a child works out how to do something. It shows trust that she'll manage.	• Ask a student how she would like a good piece of work acknowledged other than with your written comment, if at all.
• Saying something's great before it has been achieved is false and can imply there is pressure to get it right. However, showing appreciation of endeavor thus far suggests that that is good enough.	• Accumulate small achievements to justify a bigger splash of recognition. Three achievements in one week or in one term could earn different rewards.
• Children feel pride and pleasure not when they receive phony feedback about their brilliance, but when they know they worked hard and have something significant to show for it.	• For young girls, a week, or even a day, is long enough. Older girls can relate to improvements over a longer period.

73 | Praise girls' passion and purpose

A UNESCO report, *International Commission on Education for the Twenty-first Century,* identifies four kinds of learning: learning to know; learning to live together; learning to be; and learning to do.

Schools focus mostly on learning to know, and it is what girls know, or rather seem not to know, that upsets parents most. Yet learning also entails finding out about oneself: discovering personal passions, personal styles, and a sense of purpose—the "learning to do and be." These will take any girl further in life than dutiful delivery. Initiative is to be supported, even if at the start mistakes are made. Instead of gasping with frustration or outrage at the risk taken, it can be commended. Focus on whether sensible preparations were made to deal with any possible dangers or difficulties.

Occasionally, a daughter's passion and purpose will lead her into lies and wrongdoing. She may claim she went somewhere different, spend money on something she agreed not to, or listen to her friends rather than you. Understand that she could be struggling with competing demands and lures (though of course these must be legal), not being defiant.

Parents	Teachers
• Having opportunities to work with friends, even if they gossip and seem to be "off task" some of the time, can benefit learning through enhancing language and social and communication skills.	• If you have class awards, don't forget to acknowledge humor or other social attributes.
• Learning is inevitably a social activity. It never happens in a vacuum. It always involves listening, interacting with a teacher, responding to peers' and teachers' expectations, and testing and reshaping "self" assumptions in the light of the reactions of others. Social confidence can encourage more confident work.	• Encourage girls to feel comfortable in group-based projects in which they take the lead and share their ideas.
	• Find out what individual girls feel passionate about, and enable them to give presentations about these passions.
	• "Groupthink" is greater than the sum of its parts. Demonstrate through an exercise that ideas can deepen and strengthen when people work together.

74 Let the teacher do the teaching

Parents always expect higher than what you do. When you're pleased with something, they always find something wrong with it. It makes me upset.

—Debbie, age 11

When young children are proud of something they have done, of course they want to show it to us. Rather than burst their bubble of confidence with critical comments, we should aim to appreciate the piece of work and accept that they are pleased with it. If we spot something wrong or something we feel could have been done better—as we're almost bound to, being adults—we have to think carefully about how and whether to say anything. It is, essentially, for the teacher, who knows the standard expected for our child's age, to do the teaching.

If our daughter asks us to check it over, we can be more straightforward, but always having first commented positively on something we liked about the work and having checked that she is ready to hear any suggestions for changes. Some children will be happy to dive back in; others may decide they will leave it as it is, nonetheless, and this is their choice.

Parents	Teachers

- Get too critical, and your daughter won't let you near to help at all.

- Avoid changing anything or adding finishing touches as she'll no longer see it as her work.

- Only the teacher can know what to expect from a girl of her age, what is really being tested in the homework, or what's best for her to learn next.

- If there is a big difference between what she produces at home and in class, consult rather than berate the teacher. The problem could be a talkative friend, boredom, disruptive classmates, or feeling different if she does her best.

- Parents who complain are parents who care. Go easy on them, and try not to take complaints personally.

- Guidance for parents on helping with homework issued at the start of the school year may help to set the groundwork for any future discussions.

75

Every day can't be judgment day

I don't like my mom coming to watch me play. One time recently she said, "You could have played better." But we won 13–1, so what more did she want?
—Tamara, age 11

If our bosses were to check us over each day and give us daily marks out of ten, we'd end up ragged and neurotic. That's how children must feel when they are regaled with constant expressions of pleasure and disapproval. They will find it hard to find that all-important necessary private space when they feel watched continuously. Boys tend to grab the private time they need quite openly. Girls are more surreptitious and secretive and will carve it out in more dangerous ways, through not eating or lying or keeping information back. If parents are too inquisitive and judgmental about each day's events and efforts, a child may decide to give nothing away at all and either clam up or tell a load of manufactured stories.

Parents	Teachers
• Encouragement contains no judgment. It leaves your daughter feeling free to take herself forward in her own way.	• Make earning any "nice job" stickers fun.
• Use encouraging comments to help her feel you're appreciating rather than judging:	

Use encouraging comments to help her feel you're appreciating rather than judging:

—"You've put so much effort into that!"

—"I wish I'd done such interesting things at school."

—"It's hard for you but you will crack it."

• Take away any guilt or shame she might feel if she anticipates judgment: "That wasn't at all like you. Let's put it behind us and start again tomorrow."

76

Show interest but don't be intrusive

In some ways, I'd prefer my mom to understand more about what I do in my sport. But I also like it that she doesn't. I have space and more independence, and it's my thing.

—Lisa, age 10

One mom who held a very high-powered job said she was not going to attend the parent-teacher night at her daughter's school because it was the teachers' job to get the teaching right, not hers. How wrong she was! Of course, we should be interested in our child's progress and happiness in all areas of development at school. For all schoolchildren, school is almost as important as their family; for older children, it is probably more important.

But we have a dilemma. After the age of eight or so, children relish school as the place where they can be themselves and get up to a little mischief away from the often intense gaze of their parents' constant scrutiny. They need some privacy. Their need for praise from us becomes offset gradually by their need for autonomy. When girls want our appreciation, they'll tell us all we need to know.

Parents	Teachers
• Ask open-ended questions that allow your daughter to withhold detail. "Did anything good or bad happen today?" not "Who did you play with and what happened?" And start by talking about *your* day.	• Show interest in each girl's personal passions or hobbies but step back if she seems uncomfortable.
• Ask casually about grades. "That tricky math homework, how did it come out?" rather than "What mark did you get? Will I be pleased?"	• Her family experiences influence a girl a great deal. It is important to understand and acknowledge these but also to treat anything you learn with respect, as many children prefer this information to remain private.
• If you overhear talk of a difficulty, offer to discuss it but don't demand details.	• At parent-teacher events and in newsletters, stress the important role that parents can play in being encouraging about schoolwork and being interested in any developments in the school.
• Make sure your questions are genuine, not designed to find out something else.	
• Take an interest in her work, but don't take it over and do it.	

The horrendous danger in our A-grade obsession is that we are imposing labels on plants that are still growing.

—Dr. Martin Stephen, school principal

The process of getting there is as important as arriving, and along the road there should always be hope. Girls give up either because they have been told over and over again that they are a hopeless case or because they doubt their capacity to do well for other reasons. The message many hear is demoralizing and undermining: "You won't if you don't . . . "; "You will never if you carry on . . . "; or "You're a born loser, never had any success with . . . " Rather than risk further failure and have salt rubbed in already torn egos, many will decide not to try. Labels tend to stick and act as straitjackets, which will make it difficult for a girl to escape the destiny she hears described.

Girls need to hear far more upbeat and hopeful messages that will not only boost their self-belief but also make any target seem manageable and easy to keep up once achieved; for example, "Of course this is hard, but just take it one step at a time and you'll have no problem"; "You've managed to stay close and not run off from the vegetable section all the way to the meat. It's not so far now to the checkout. Did you think it would be this easy? I knew you could do it!"

Parents	Teachers

- Remind your daughter of past successes so she can think positively and believe in herself.

- If success appears unfamiliar or scary and seems to carry heavy responsibilities for continuing in the same vein, it may be easier for a girl to remain the devil she knows.

- If she sets herself a goal that she's failed to complete before, don't remind her of the past failure. Greet each resolution as a first, and stay positive.

- Motivation is grounded in hope and experience.

- Sarcasm and ridicule usually puncture hope. Don't use them.

- Make sure that a girl's hope is grounded in a practical reality. Help her to put together a plan.

- Break the challenge down into small, manageable chunks, and remind her of difficulties she has previously overcome.

- Never say what one teacher said to a mother: "Your daughter is destined for a life of failure if she continues this way."

78 Encourage girls to make links and connections

Creative thinking expands children's horizons and is fun, because it produces surprises. It encourages girls to see new ways of doing things and to solve problems, which should enable them to feel more confident and capable. Parents and teachers can mitigate girls' tendency to play safe and avoid intellectual adventure by making it a familiar family or classroom practice to find and enjoy unusual links between ideas, events, and products or between one topic area and another. Of course, it is also important to go easy on the criticism.

Many people believe that children start out more creative and resourceful because they have not become locked into set ways of seeing things through the pressure to conform, the desire to please, or the constraints of logic. It is a shame to see the spirit and individuality of a child diminish when she has to fit the formality of an organized classroom, but her creativity will not be irretrievably lost if we avoid overemphasizing the benefit of being "good" (so don't ask, "Have you been a good girl today?") and applaud her imagination and ability to see links. If something goes wrong, such as a cake sinking in the middle or a clay pot collapsing, better to laugh and liken it to something else altogether than focus on the "failure."

Parents	Teachers

- Cartoonists exploit unusual connections and generate humor from the unexpected. Collect cartoons from newspapers and magazines in a scrapbook and laugh at them together.

- Encourage making connections from an early age. Make events trigger familiar songs or stories; say, "Now that reminds me of when . . . "

- Number links can be made by comparisons of the dots and symbols on dice, playing cards, and dominoes.

- Play word association and alphabet games when you walk and travel.

- Don't get upset by mess when she is creating or experimenting.

- Be understanding of work that's not quite what you had in mind, provided it is thought through and demonstrates understanding. The student could be a future Nobel Prize winner!

- Avoid commanding total obedience in every way. Allow girls to joke about funny things that come to mind, even if they verge on being fresh.

- Girls who are naturally timid and like to be told exactly what to do should be encouraged to experiment, and those who enjoy experimentation need sometimes to stick to what's expected.

Two steps forward, one back

Learning anything is a strange business, for it rarely happens in a predictable way or to a set pattern. Children learn, mature, and develop in phases and spurts, and each child will manage it in her unique way. Girls get "eureka" moments when everything falls into place, but then they can get quite scared and may want to return to the time they were more dependent and needed to rely on help. That way, they don't risk being wrong. At each stage of advance, they can feel quite exposed. Learning, therefore, is often a case of two steps forward, one step back, as the knowledge or new behavior begins to feel normal.

In relation to behavior, a girl often needs to test parental reactions after she has been accommodating for a while, to check if her parents really have become cooler and kinder and won't revert to being harsh or frightening if she slips up again. If parents ride the highs and lows because this is understood, this is a form of acceptance and affirmation that has the same effect as giving direct praise.

We may also witness "two steps back, three great leaps forward." Younger children can appear to go into reverse before they make a significant developmental advance—their brains seem to take a vacation before they then go full speed ahead.

Parents	Teachers

Parents

- When a girl needs to tread water for a while and take time out from the pressure of eternal "progress," she should certainly not be frowned upon or punished.

- If your daughter seems to have "lost it" and become confused or cannot do something she could before, wait patiently. Within a week she is likely to have rediscovered the ability and made a significant advance.

- Children learn by doing; they also learn by sleeping on it, imagining it, "playing with" the idea, and thinking it through subconsciously. Don't ask for minute evidence of step-by-step learning.

Teachers

- Curriculum targets and standardized tests assume that every child is developing as the "average" when each one progresses uniquely.

- Try to include some flexibility in the study program.

- Give a girl who is flagging evidence that she is not stupid, merely working on the problem in her way and at her own speed.

- Try to convince her that she'll catch up, and confirm that, as in any investment, "past performance is no guarantee of future outcomes"!

80 | Pick one thing at a time

When parents reach the end of their tether because everything a child does seems to make life difficult, the temptation is to complain about everything at once and tackle all the issues in one offensive. This can be the worst response because it rarely works, and it leaves a child despondent and confused.

It is hard for any young child to hold lots of rules and expectations in her or his head at once. It is also likely that constant nagging and criticism will be seen as a sign by self-doubting girls up to the age of eight or so that they're no good because they're unable to please. As has been said, until a child has a strong and separate sense of self, she cannot be convinced that a complaint about how she has behaved is not a complaint directed at her as a person.

Everyone benefits by picking one aspect of behavior to turn around at a time. The chances of success are higher, the nagging and edginess are reduced, and life is more generally relaxed. Most valuable, once things have improved on the central problem, other challenging behavior tends to disappear as a result of fewer fights, less resentment, and a higher profile of praise and encouragement.

Parents	Teachers

Parents

- Don't pile on the demands or the complaints; this can cause tempers to flare.

- Identify the behavior that bugs you most or the time of day that is most trying, and start there. Drop the nagging about other problems until the top priority is sorted out.

- Let your daughter know that this is your plan, and make it seem like a fair contract: She does her bit and you do yours, which is staying cool about other matters.

- For schoolwork, suggest that she work to improve one subject at a time. Don't ask her to pull out all the stops on her reading and her math, or her science and her history, at the same time.

Teachers

- With a challenging class, reflect upon the source of the main problem—a handful of particularly disruptive students, classroom management (because they sit and disrupt together), or teaching style (because some seem to lose interest very quickly). Pick on the most plausible explanation and unravel that problem first.

- Give girls who struggle clear and achievable short-term goals so they know exactly where they must focus and see the way forward. When one does well, make sure she knows and accepts that it was her knowledge and understanding that got her there, not chance.

Chapter 10

The Perils of Perfectionism

M any people have become concerned that an increasing pressure to achieve and do well has led
to more high-flying students' becoming perfectionists
and "success junkies," dependent on their regular fix of
achievement and accolades, success and celebration,
without which they feel incomplete. For example, the
former dean of Harvard undergraduate college, Harry
Lewis, was openly concerned by some students' need to
impress and to receive acknowledgment and rewards
for everything when he wrote to students, "You may
balance your life better if you participate in some activities purely for fun. . . . Many of the most important
and rewarding things that you do will be recorded on
no piece of paper but only as imprints on your mind
and soul."

Whereas some children seem able to survive, even
thrive on, pressure, others may develop an unhealthy
level of perfectionism that conceals considerable self-
doubt and distress because they often pursue impossible
goals and are never satisfied with the result. Girls seem
particularly prone to this pattern, and sometimes respond by developing an eating disorder or self-harming,
but boys succumb, too.

What attitudes and support help to keep children free of turmoil and competitive anxiety? Research shows that children who aim high, do well, and can sustain success in a healthy and balanced way work to their own, realistic, and flexible, standards and expectations. They can take on both mistakes and failure. They tend to be well organized, to have uncritical parents, and to strive for their own benefit because they enjoy the activity. They are in control. Most important, they have a robust and stable self-esteem that doesn't rely on proving themselves to others or coming out on top to buoy them up.

The seeds of unhealthy perfectionism take root where, in the eyes of the child, approval appears conditional on success; where children strive to meet very high and inflexible expectations that they see others hold for them; where adults take the credit for, or "steal," any success; where no success ever seems good enough because targets always shift; where constant challenge generates constant doubt about ability; and where success is lauded, failure is shunned, and fear of failure is intense. So perfectionist attitudes do not help children to be happy, despite the often impressive achievements that accumulate: One setback will suggest a future strewn with failure.

If parents overemphasize being successful from an early age, girls can become obsessed with doing well because they believe parental approval depends on it. Constant striving reinforces their doubt about any success ever being good enough. This self-doubt and the associated anxiety may result in burnout or opting out—the opposite of what parents want! The tips that follow suggest how to help girls develop healthier attitudes toward both success and failure.

Everyone Gets Scars on the Way to the Stars
—Title of a song by Fran Landesman, jazz singer

Parents and teachers are often tempted to ask a child to go that extra mile and are loath to make the target easier if the child then struggles. If a problem appears, it tends to be interpreted as attitude and application, not an unrealistic target.

Research shows that being able to be flexible and to compromise on standards and targets is one of the keys to healthy striving. If a girl begins to set tough targets and beats herself up emotionally if she doesn't quite get there, encourage her to go easy. Of course it's great if she does very well, but it is more important that she not find herself in the stranglehold of a perfectionist straitjacket.

Parents	Teachers
• Never berate your daughter for having not quite excelled, even as a joke.	• A girl who frequently misses deadlines may be trying to perform at too high a standard to prove something. Discuss with colleagues how best to readjust her standards and encourage her to be content with work achieved in less time.
• How perfectionist are you? Try to demonstrate flexibility in your own goal setting.	
• Don't harbor inflexible goals for your daughter.	• Make it clear that each student achieves at a different level, but that high performance should not come at the expense of enriching leisure time or peace of mind.

82 Don't make approval conditional on a girl's success

I was thrilled when my nine-year-old daughter won the English prize at her school. She continued to do really well throughout the next year, and I was waiting for her to receive the prize again come summer. She didn't get it. I found myself being short with her and putting her down quite a bit. I'm a successful professional woman, and I'm astonished that I felt my disappointment that deeply and that I took it out on her.

At least this mom admitted her feelings. Her first reaction—of vindictive disappointment—is more common than anyone would care to accept, although her subsequent insight is far less usual. If we expect good things, it is very easy to feel disappointed and let down if they do not happen, but no child should suffer the burden of believing that success is the only way to maintain either her parents' love or their approval.

We might have a similar reaction if our daughter behaved badly on an occasion that mattered to us and we felt shown up. If we "went cold" on her but did not actually reprimand her for a specific wrongdoing, we could be falling into the trap of reserving our approval for times when she makes us feel good.

Parents	Teachers
• Accept that it is not good for your daughter to aim to be perfect, and that every experience, including every setback, is an important stepping-stone in learning and growing.	• Treat all students fairly, without favoritism. Accept each one as a worthwhile individual; don't reserve your enthusiasm for the accommodating and successful ones.
• See the funny side and the alternative potential of any shortfalls.	• Show that you value a wide range of attitudes, specialist knowledge, and skills. Refer to past achievements and anticipate future ones.
• If you find yourself being disappointed by a second-best outcome, remind yourself that you are not her and she is not you. In your mind, draw a boundary between you and her, and resolve to stop living parasitically through her.	• Focus on the process as well as the outcome. How the improvement was achieved is the aspect to highlight, rather than the success itself.
	• Encourage all students to make important decisions and take responsibility for these, so each one feels trusted by you.

83 Let a girl take, and keep, the ownership of her success

Children need to keep possession of any success and realize that it's theirs. No one else should run off and tell the world, as if it was their achievement and their prize.

—Head teacher and
special-educational-needs expert

Of course, our daughter owns her success, but it is very easy to take it over and thereby take it from her. That is what we are doing when we use it to make us feel successful. We feel so thrilled by the achievement that we are almost driven to run off with it and show it to all our friends. We can get enormous kudos when our children do very well in their various activities.

But if we effectively steal her success and spread around any special news, rather than feeling fulfilled our daughter could be left feeling empty and bereft. She could then feel driven to replenish the success, over and over again.

Parents	Teachers

- Personal success should be seen as the child's property, not the parent's. You would not consider borrowing anything of your daughter's without asking, and the same courtesy should apply here.

- Check first whether she wishes anyone else to know, and if she would like to tell any particular people herself.

- Asking her not only shows you respect her and her wishes but also makes the success unambiguously hers.

- Devaluing something that she believes to be a success also "steals" the achievement and pleasure from her: "But a third of the class got that mark. That's not so special!"

- When schools use children's achievements to pump up their prospectuses, there is a danger that students will feel used.

84 Stay in touch with a girl's reality

Don't be arrogant enough to assume you always know what a girl wants and how she feels. It is important to keep talking and giving her the opportunity to discuss her fears and feelings freely with you, including those that could hurt or disappoint you.

She must be free to talk about shame, letting you down, always having hankered after some other activity than the one you encouraged, or her fear of failure and perhaps distorted imaginings. There will be pluses to discuss, too: which aspects of her life give her the most pleasure, how she rates each of her talents or particular skills.

For example, if you celebrate a child's success, the event should suit her, not you. A ten-year-old could find it hard to relate to a horde of neighbors or relatives descending on you, talking to each other, and enjoying alcohol. You may enjoy adult company, but she may prefer to be alone or with friends her age. If that's the case, of what benefit was the gathering to her?

Parents	Teachers

- Plan any celebration at your daughter's level, not the way you would mark some notable feat of your own.

- Take her worries seriously. Don't ignore something that saddens or annoys her.

- If you refuse to see things her way and impose your view, she could lose touch with herself and become your reflection.

- Younger children make sense of things in surprising ways and readily believe in the unbelievable, such as Santa Claus and tooth fairies. Just because you know why something has to be, it does not follow that she also understands.

- Try to uncover any worries that lie behind late, "lost," or very poor work. There could be distress at home, or a girl could fear demonstrating her total lack of understanding and so not bother at all.

- Appreciate that strong parental antagonism to school and study could dilute a girl's commitment to work. It is a conflicting reality for her, and she's likely to struggle with the conflict.

85 Talk about "development," not "improvement"

Girls who have the opportunity to discover new interests, talents, and skills learn more about themselves and establish a pattern of self-discovery that can enrich the rest of their lives. Self-discovery is, indeed, the main purpose: Only if they explore what is there inside can they discover their true potential and experience the thrill and excitement that lies in store. The process should be one of self-development, not self-improvement.

Improvement implies that a girl is progressively better and more clever than how she was before. It suggests that how she was before was not "right"; yet, to repeat, she needs to see her past as an acceptable part of her. The subtle message could be that she needs to go on getting better and improving herself, trying one new thing after another in order to remain acceptable. We should not demand that she fulfill her potential, because we can never know what potential is there or when it is fulfilled. Better to ask her to unpeel a layer or two of possible resistance to reveal her reserve of capability—for her own enjoyment.

Parents	Teachers
• Make it clear that it is the results or the technique that is improving, not your daughter's personality or "self."	• Separate the girl from the improvement. Refer to her understanding deepening, to her application becoming more effective, to her new inspiration or her growing skill at identifying reference materials or with a technique, rather than marveling at her generalized "improvement."
• Talk about discovery, rather than improvement: "You're discovering all sorts of new things about yourself!" "You're discovering you can feel comfortable with math after all"; "Did you think you could pull out those extra stops and speed up your sprint time so successfully?"	

86 Don't be wowed by neatness

There is a pattern. The girls who develop eating disorders are such perfectionists. Their handwriting is so neat and their work presented beautifully. They are always the "good," caring girls.

—A high school counselor

Work that is neat and well presented might seem to suggest that the student is on top of things, thinking carefully, not rushing, and taking pride in her work, but it could be a mistake to see the perfect presentation as a sign that all's well—for it might not be.

Neatness can be contrived as a diversion from content, with a girl believing the words alone to be not quite good enough; it can be used as a tactic to impress both the teacher and fellow students, to make her work look perfect as well as being pleasing in itself—the makeup and lipstick applied lovingly to the assignment, just as she may strive to look perfect.

Of course, neatness can imply simply that a student has a natural orderly approach to work that may be time-saving, not time-consuming, so it may not conceal deeper doubts, but if a girl is taking so long over work that playtime gets lost and bedtime gets delayed, it's better not to praise the presentation but to encourage spreading her interests and using her time more sensibly.

Parents	Teachers

- Focus on the content, not on the presentation, and encourage your daughter to appraise it. Ask, "But what do you think of it? You're the best judge of what you've written."

- Try to encourage her to be specific: "You said you did badly. What was it you thought didn't go right?" or, "Yes, I liked what you did, but what pleased you in particular?"

- Such details help you to assess the accuracy or health of her judgment.

- Before her report card is due, ask her for her best guess of what will be included.

- Invite students to moderate each other's work, having first discussed what points, skills, and understanding needed to be covered. The judgment that any girl applies to another's work will be fresh to apply to her own. The value of presentation should also be assessed.

- If you think that someone's neatness could be approaching an obsession, make it clear you like to see words crossed out and don't like headings underlined in different colors and might mark her down if she persists.

87 Don't constantly move the goalposts

I'd done very well in school, and outside in music, dance, swimming, and so on. I'd loved doing those things, but I was conscious they'd all been organized by my parents. I felt I was having to live up to the expectations that other people had of me. I had the sense of being misunderstood, and therefore out of control. I had a double life, my successful public persona and my inside person, who was not very happy and not sure what she really wanted.

—Anita, age 21

Demanding schools and parents are prone to move the goalposts. As soon as one target is in sight and therefore appears easy, another more challenging one is presented to prevent any flagging of effort. Or as soon as one goal has been reached, another is put in its place to maintain the momentum: "If you can achieve that, then surely this is also within reach!"

But even a successful girl who coasts through challenges should take breaks from constant achievement and have a greater degree of control over her life and commitments. If she says, "No, that's enough," that is healthy, and her wishes should be respected.

Parents	Teachers
• Challenges must tempt girls to discover themselves, not threaten them, put them off, or make them feel inadequate until they fulfill them.	• Factor in the child's view of what she can, and wants to, achieve, and put her in control as far as is practical to reduce the pressure.
• When girls are allowed to select the moment to renew their efforts, their readiness reflects their confidence.	• Asking for perfect answers and work before moving someone on encourages perfectionist attitudes.
• Shifting goalposts represent a broken deal. Girls can store up resentment, self-doubt, and anxiety.	

88 | Accept good-enough success

Growing up feeling my best wasn't good enough encouraged me to become defiant and stop trying. But although I appeared no longer to care, I continued to beat myself up inside for being useless.

—Amanda, age 16

Any girl faced with successive mirage-style targets as discussed in the previous tip—ones that disappear as you approach, like the shimmering "puddles" of water on hot roads on sunny days—will very likely conclude that no success is good enough. If no success, however great, is good enough, a child will never know if she is good enough or, indeed, if she is any good at all. This is a very uncomfortable thought, so she will need to achieve more success to convince herself that she is good enough and worthy of praise. Success, if sought for this reason, will not raise self-esteem or self-belief, nor will it deepen the self-concept. At worst, it deepens self-doubt; at best, it leaves someone's self-esteem vulnerable and prone to fluctuation.

Self-belief comes not from a sense that we are perfect, but from the knowledge that we are good enough but have more to give.

Parents	Teachers

Parents

- Lead your daughter when she's ready. For success to benefit self-worth, a girl needs time to absorb the achievement, to be sure she can repeat it, and to make it part of her identity. Only she can know when she is ready.

- Being pushed to move on too soon generates considerable anxiety, a noted characteristic of perfectionists who feel driven by others.

- Good-enough success is not a cop-out—accepting second best or laziness. It is the result of honest (though perhaps not top-notch) striving that produced real progress and is the guard against either internal or external pressure.

Teachers

- Let all success be good enough, at least for a time, including your own.

- Ask your students when they are ready to make an extra push to raise their grades or enter a competition.

- Untidy work can be considered good enough if the content is sound. Find out why the work was apparently rushed; if it was to create time to fit in other valuable activities, it could be a sensible trade-off.

Mother: *Do up your shoelaces! You might trip and fall over.*

Daughter: *What's the matter? Can't you take a risk?*

—Rebecca, age 10

This episode shows how easy it is to convey in small ways that taking risks is not a good idea. This girl's response was unusual, for girls are often more risk-averse than boys. They don't like to be scolded, and they like to play by the rules most of the time and not leave too much to chance, preferring to overprepare rather than skimp on study. Some develop an attitude described as *learned helplessness,* where they claim incompetence and court as much help and guidance as they can elicit to reduce the risk of getting something wrong.

The ability to take risks is important, for learning is a risky business. Coming down hard when she's risked something and misjudged it could lead a girl to avoid larger risks. Girls with perfectionist tendencies have very high standards. Fear of falling short tempts some to self-handicap to avoid the anxiety, consciously or unconsciously. A girl may put things off until it is too late or aim ridiculously high to ensure failure or too low so the result means nothing. She may destroy her work; she may even cheat to ensure the outcome. Some develop inexplicable lethargy, pains, or eating disorders, any of which provide an excuse to exit the proverbial rat race.

Parents	Teachers

Parents

- Talk honestly about any mistakes you might have made in the past and any you make now. Let your daughter see that risks often pay off and there's always something to learn even if they don't.

- Encourage her to face her fears, not run from them.

- Adventurous play that incorporates a measure of planned physical risk or that confronts the unexpected is helpful.

- Promote self-direction. Don't solve every problem for her and become overprotective.

Teachers

- If you make a mistake, be open and honest about it.

- Raise class awareness of differing attitudes toward mistakes by initiating a discussion. Observe any gender patterns, and talk about them.

- Girls are often more timid and don't relish competitive games. Invite students to reflect upon what winning, losing, or participating means to them.

- Girls with low self-belief have neither the courage to take chances nor the confidence to change. Strive to strengthen self-belief.

Don't ignore or punish failure

If they only tell you the good things, you don't get the truth.

—Caitlin, age 11

Parents are often advised to encourage children by ignoring mistakes and focusing on what they do well. This helps girls when they are very young, when they find it hard to control either their bodies or their feelings, when they take the first steps in learning and are too young to live within wall-to-wall rules. However, as they mature, they should be honest about the quality and effect of their work and behavior. But girls tend to take criticism to heart, so mistakes must be discussed extremely carefully. If parents continue to disregard failures while celebrating successes, the hidden message can be that failure is shameful and must be avoided. This view is certainly typical of perfectionists.

Failure is not something to be shunned or punished. It provides factual and neutral information on what went wrong, what has not been understood fully, and on what needs to be changed. The experience of failure becomes shameful when a child has invested her self-worth in doing well, or when a parent relies on a daughter's success for personal satisfaction and happiness, so failure becomes associated with disappointment and discomfort.

Parents	Teachers
• Respond sensitively to setbacks.	• If any girl tries to hide a disappointing result or cries if she gets less than the highest mark or fails to make the top three, ask to speak to her parents to discuss what might lie behind her self-criticism.
• If your daughter's failures become your personal shame, or if her successes lift you from gloom, you make it harder for her.	
• Help her to see where the problem lies: She hadn't understood something because she rushed at it or because the subject is not her forte. Perhaps she has overambitious standards. The problem is *not* that *she* is useless. Make her move beyond self-flagellation.	• Failure can be seen to undermine a girl's mission to be "good" and please significant others. Help to take the shame out of any failure, and clarify the lessons to be learned.
• See failure as neutral. It is not appropriate to rub her nose in it or tease her.	• Hear her side of the story.
• Making mistakes can show she is working at the frontier of her knowledge and understanding, so be tolerant.	

Chapter 11

Praise and You

Having spoken to countless adults over the years, to people who have been successful as well as to those leading less remarkable lives, I found it surprising how many were quick to volunteer that their parents, and particularly their fathers, never praised them. They never felt their efforts were appreciated and were left with a feeling that they were simply not good enough or not sufficiently interesting personalities to be noticed. This experience has influenced the course of the lives of some, for they are still trying to please even though the parent is no longer around to watch the show. It remains unfinished business, and while this urge may lead to higher achievement than a more contented childhood might have delivered, the success masks an eternal sadness, sense of letdown, and underlying restlessness.

One acquaintance, who is now a leading politician and active in government, agreed that her desire to prove herself as good as her brothers in the eyes of her father had generated her need to do well and make a mark from a young age. One man who sits at the top of his profession readily acknowledged the importance of self-esteem and said he had suffered quietly all his life because his father had neither praised him nor appeared to recognize or value his talents. As a consequence, he was happy now to be able to work with young students and graduates to encourage them to strengthen their sense of self through acquiring wider experiences of which they could feel proud.

Someone who experienced difficulty at the other end of the range of parental behavior is a young woman who showed early musical talent and was expected to meet demanding practice and performance schedules as a result, to make music her career. She was praised, but grudgingly and with conditions attached. Her success was never good enough. She felt increasingly that her life was not her own and that the only way to regain control was to give up. From that day, she never touched her instrument again.

It is surprising that so many people have been so honest, for adults more commonly deny the importance of the things they weren't lucky enough to have or, alternatively, state that something potentially unpleasant that did happen had no lasting ill effect. The conclusion has to be that the impact on children, young or older, of living either without apparent parental pleasure, acknowledgment, or recognition, or with parents who push too hard to gain something for them, is clearly profound: It is a pattern that we should ensure will not be repeated.

91 | Unblock your blocks to giving praise

Many people find it very hard to give praise. Some feel uncomfortable with using the unfamiliar words; some simply do not know what to praise; and others squirm with disapproval at—or are deeply skeptical of—the whole process. The most common reasons people have to justify being sparing with praise include:

- that it can easily make a girl bigheaded;
- that praise should be given only for "excellence": outstanding achievement and effort beyond expectation;
- that if something could be better, it should not be praised, as the praise could encourage laziness and send the wrong messages about general standards and expectations;
- that a girl should be doing well in every sphere before she is rewarded, in case she takes a slide in an activity a parent thinks really matters;
- that the parents created the success, not the girl, because they enforced the study regime or paid for extra tuition, for example;
- that previously it has had no impact, so they dropped it.

Some mothers may be slow to praise academic or other success if it rouses jealousy, makes them feel inferior, or sharpens regret about missed opportunities.

Parents	Teachers

- Reflect on your childhood experiences and your current attitudes toward giving and receiving praise. What has been your strongest influence?

- Think hard to detect any difference in your treatment of girls and boys.

- If you work outside the home, how do you praise people there, if at all? Do you have the same approach at home? If not, why not?

- Give as you receive. When your daughter shows you affection and regard (both can be considered praise), make sure you reciprocate.

- Reflect on your past, at home and at school, and ponder on any patterns you could be repeating.

- Consider whether you find it easier to respond encouragingly in the classroom or at home with your own family, and think through why it might be so.

Ask for praise if you want to hear it

If you do not receive much positive feedback from your family, at work, or from your friends, it is likely that you have learned to do without it. Men tend to be more self-sufficient—or like to consider themselves so—and may not even notice its absence. Women are more praise-hungry in childhood and are also more likely to miss getting pats on the back as adults.

If you want to hear it, ask for it; most "significant others" are willing to be supportive once they realize that partners or friends want some backup. Very few will refuse you. Children can be encouraged to be appreciative after you have done something well, not just to be polite but as a genuine recognition of the special effort or achievement.

Those who think they can do without praise and consider it a big fuss about not very much will almost certainly find it harder to offer it to others. They may also think that for boys, especially, praise is unnecessary and that girls should learn to grow up less needy of other people's approval. The best way to encourage a reluctant partner to become freer with his or her appreciation toward a child of yours is to take a back route and praise and appreciate the partner overtly first.

Parents	Teachers

- Be specific. Analyze what you'd like to have more of, for example, appreciation of your efforts or talents or acceptance of your views and values; then go and ask for it.

- Children tend to take what is done for them, at any level, as "normal parenting." It's hard for them to see that less might be done for them, so don't be harsh about their apparent insensitivity.

- It is healthier to do something because you want to (in which case, perhaps you don't need big thanks) than to curry favor. But if you'd like your efforts appreciated, describe that bit extra that you gave. Genuine thanks grow from genuine giving.

- Think which job you consider you do well and whose appreciation you would value. Then go and seek confirmation and reinforcement.

- Positive feedback can come from colleagues, students, and parents. How might each of these show their appreciation? What might you be entitled to expect?

93 | If you did something well, believe it

In a world that seems obsessed with excellence, especially achievements that deliver big financial rewards, it can be hard to feel any pride in less obvious successes—or to realize that is what they are despite their modest scale.

People at work are increasingly being encouraged to identify and acknowledge their strengths and achievements. These might be relatively minor, such as responding sensitively to a junior member of the staff who came in with a problem but left with a lighter step and a plan of action. In the home environment, there's no boss to offer compliments on your efforts that day, no daily target to meet. But we have good moments and successes nonetheless, and there are hundreds of tasks to be done, with or without our children, that involve the same efficiency skills, conflict resolution, stress management, and practical and communication and listening skills that are on show in the workplace.

Looking at what we did and did well—rather than at what we did not do—and feeling pleased about it will act as a boost and help us to be positive and encouraging with our daughters and partners.

Parents	Teachers

- An appreciative daughter is one who smiles, is happy, and shows affection to you. And sometimes she actually says thanks.

- If you feel uncomfortable receiving praise, learn simply to say thank you and hold onto it; don't bat it back.

- If you receive good feedback from a colleague, parent, or student about something you have done, accept that it is valid. Don't squirm and claim you do not deserve the praise or that the affirmation is uncalled for because what you did was just in the line of duty.

If you feel that you have done something impressive, either given your starting point or because it represents a significant step toward a longer-term goal, reward yourself. Whatever is your special treat, allow yourself to have or do it.

The reward can be something you enjoy alone, or it could be something you choose to share with one other person. It might be sitting down with an easy-to-read trashy book, watching a film or DVD during the day, taking a long, scented bath, having a drink with a friend, or watching the sports channels all day one weekend.

Marking an achievement with a reward helps you to acknowledge that you got there, so you are entitled to take a break; it proves that you are not compelled always to go that one step farther before you allow yourself to feel pleased; and it enables you to understand how your children might also value each small gesture of appreciation and feel their effort was worthwhile.

Parents	Teachers

- Think of things you might enjoy doing in any spare time, such as taking a walk or spending time in the yard. Remember these when you feel you deserve a small, or larger, treat.

- The best reward is your own satisfaction; then there are no ifs and buts floating around in your head. Practice saying to yourself, "That was a great job! I can be really pleased about that."

- Rewards don't always have to benefit you. You can share a treat or treat someone else if that gives you pleasure.

- Reflect on the times during an inevitably pressured day that you might enjoy some respite when you feel you deserve it.

- Remember good-enough success. Making a special effort, even if things didn't go entirely as planned, is worth marking; otherwise you might not try again!

95 | Accept any praise given to you

If someone praises you, accept the praise and hold onto it. Don't squirm with discomfort or hand it back as soon as you can with the words "It was nothing very special," "I'm not sure what I've done to deserve a comment like that," or "I was going to do it anyway." Girls and women are particularly prone to such self-denigration. They may have tried hard, but they usually believe that they should have done that anyway, which makes the effort seem commonplace, not worthy of comment.

If you often feel you don't deserve any recognition or accolades and you instead feel embarrassed when someone tells you you have done well, you may imagine others feel the same, including your child. This makes it more likely you will be sparing with your praise, to protect her from the expected discomfort.

But this reticence is not helpful. Far better to change your mind-set and learn to accept positive feedback with good grace when you are fortunate enough to receive it!

Parents	Teachers
• Practice saying thank you when you are given praise, and teach your daughter to do the same.	• If any student says, "That was fun!" or "That was interesting," respond with a thank you rather than "good." Her comment is intended as complimentary feedback, not to make you realize she enjoyed it.
• Don't make a joke about giving or hearing praise until everyone in the family knows that, mostly, it is given straight and can be trusted. Only then is it safe to lighten things with a bit of fun, and then only on the odd occasion.	

Don't compete with your daughter

My mother was so competitive with all of us daughters. She always had to claim that she knew more than us, could do things faster than us, had read this book or that one by the time she was our age, had traveled as much, and, later, that her marriage was more successful than ours. It was so sad and probably meant that she felt very insecure, but during my childhood, it made me feel she could never be proud of me. It also made it hard to be proud of myself.

—Heidi, 25

Avoid competing with your daughter. Some mothers and fathers find it hard to give their children the space to become better than, more beautiful than, more skilled than themselves. But growing girls need to feel respected for their achievements, not constantly pushed into a parent's shadow.

Parents	Teachers
• Your becoming competitive is more likely to switch your daughter off than to spur her to greater effort, as it could make her feel overpowered and dejected.	• "Know-it-all" students may become irritating, but never try to trip them up with difficult questions or be tempted to set up a competition and beat them in an exchange of knowledge.
• If you are competitive with her, she is more likely to be so with others.	
• Avoid referring to your past to claim any superior edge because you will almost certainly not have remembered the time or event accurately.	

97 | Show respect for the other parent

It is not always possible for both biological parents to live together under the same roof. However, despite the actual living arrangements, it will help any girl to work and grow healthily and happily if each parent not only is involved to some degree in her schooling and upbringing but also is shown a measure of regard by the other parent. If a father fails to compliment her mother or shows actual disrespect, a girl could find herself torn between them; she may doubt herself as a growing female or find it hard to trust males.

If her mother speaks only ill of her father, this will raise questions about how much of him lives on in her.

Parents	Teachers

- Parents need to earn the respect of their daughter as she matures and becomes more discriminating. She will gauge how well they treat each other and others and judge whether either deserves her respect.

- Watch your words and reactions as you watch movies or television together. Swearing, making catcalls, or making other derogatory remarks often implies disrespect.

- Fathers or father figures are important to girls, especially when they enter puberty, so fathers should offer plenty of love and positive feedback. Brothers, uncles, or cousins could offer alternative affirmation.

- Every school should adopt sexual harassment and antidiscrimination policies. Girls and female staff should, of course, treat their male colleagues and peers with the same respect.

- Gender awareness and equality of regard should apply throughout the school and in every lesson to help boys and girls flourish equally.

98 Enjoy your own company and that of others

The best thing about having friends is that you can assume they spend time with you because they enjoy your company. If they didn't, they wouldn't. They let you know that you are good to be around, which at times can be quite intoxicating—and of course they are also there to share your problems if you ever need them, as well as to provide a source of great fun.

Enjoying the company of your friends will help you to realize why it is good to enjoy the company of your daughter. It will help her to feel valued and to appreciate that she is someone who is able to give other people pleasure rather than be a source of disappointment and strife. These feelings will provide an enormous boost to her confidence. If you give time to your friends but also show you value and enjoy your daughter because you reserve time for her, she will get the true measure of the value you attach to her. Maintaining friendships therefore offers a double benefit, provided your friends don't crowd her out.

Parents	Teachers

Parents

- "I've had a lovely morning with my friends, and now I'm having a lovely time with you. Aren't I lucky?"

- If you take your daughter with you when you meet friends, make sure she feels involved either in the group or with something you take for her to do.

- Be careful if you collect your younger children from school that they don't feel ignored as they emerge because you are deep in conversation with others. Greet them warmly each time.

- Enjoyment is a product of engaging with the present, the here and now.

Teachers

- Enjoy your students by talking to them as you see them around the building between classes.

- Take time to enjoy yourself with colleagues in the staff room rather than working continuously.

Children reap dividends when parents are comfortable with themselves. This comfort entails accepting personal histories and the decisions that have been made, or not made, in earlier years. We should not continue to beat ourselves up for anything that happened or to put the shutters down on the past and pretend that certain events did not happen. The more content we feel with ourselves, the less we will be tempted to relive or deny things through our children, and the more we will be able to support and encourage them in healthy ways that reflect and give space to their true selves.

If we think we are not valuable or that nothing we do is ever good enough, it is tempting to fill the emptiness that we feel inside with our daughter's successes or failures, and too easy to fashion an identity based on those and to mold her to suit. We are likely to be more demanding of success and more grudging in giving praise, waiting until we feel it is really deserved. If she makes a mistake, we could feel it as a reflection on us, so we may either undervalue the importance of the event or criticize her to protect our self-image.

Parents	Teachers
• Write down your strong points.	• Write down your professional strengths, and enjoy and cherish these attributes.
• Identify your regrets. But every cloud has a silver lining; nothing is ever a total disaster. For every decision or event you regret in the past, try to identify a positive personal trait or outcome that arose from it.	• List your weaker traits, and evaluate how much they have genuinely set you back.
	• Consider how much you pressure your students to cover up your feared weaknesses.
• Think of everything you have done to help others. Achievement is not just scored by publicly accepted measures.	• Try to accept that school should help students to thrive academically and socially and to mature in many ways. Recall instances when you have helped a student to grow and develop, not just pass the exams.

Good parenting is not about perfection because it is impossible to get it absolutely right all the time. In any case, people differ in their views about what is the right, or best, response to any situation, so perfection is not a practical goal. We make mistakes as parents—lots of them—just as growing girls do. We need encouraging pats on the back for doing our best: for trying new and more positive ways to say things to our daughters, and for trying to understand more about how they think and learn and about parent-child relationship dynamics—just as girls need encouragement. Our intentions and efforts are important; and these will often be enough to bring about noticeable changes in attitude and performance that need to be noticed in order to encourage further self-enhancing changes.

The future must look enticing. We are doing well enough, and we can make changes to make the future look rosier. Our girls can and will do well, and we should help them to imagine and expect a positive future by creating an atmosphere of hope for, belief in, and appreciation of everyone in the family in the here and now.

Parents	Teachers

- Setbacks are normal—part of the ebb and flow of life. The future will be bright, and we will feel more encouraged if we apply some of the tips offered within these pages.

- Don't beat yourself up: Apply the recommended 4:1 praise to criticism or blame ratio to yourself. Each time you think you fall short, find four things to do, or that you have already done, that you can feel pleased about.

- "True power does not reveal itself" (Foucault, French philosopher). Providing a home in which each individual is empowered and able to explore her or his potential, quirks, and interests without pressure and intrusive guidance is the healthy way forward.

- Teaching is part of your life but not all of it. Think of all the other ways to accept and evaluate yourself—community or faith activist, parent, partner, son or daughter—and be positive about your overall contribution.

- Be encouraged. The future is almost always rich and rosy if you open yourself to opportunities and think positively!

Postscript

In case you have reached the end of the book and feel a little swamped and confused by the "oughts" and "buts" having read it straight through, here are some suggestions and summaries.

In the broad view, far more children suffer today from not being praised enough than are being damaged by excessive or misplaced praise. Children have a profound need not only to be noticed by the close adults in their lives but also to be affirmed, appreciated, and enjoyed. Spending time with children can be difficult when everyone is so pressured, but all efforts to do so will be amply rewarded with warmth and love from a child who feels secure and self-confident and wants to have fun as well as to do well.

It is said that we remember a maximum of 10 percent of what we hear or read at any one time. Having been faced with one hundred tips and many more bullets, you might find it helpful to sift through your thoughts by writing down ten things that have remained clear and on which you could take action confidently. Perhaps some of these could be placed on the "good things to do" side and some on the "best avoided" side. Prioritize these, try them out over a few days, and then dip into the book again to expand your repertoire from these experiences. Some will work for you, some may not. The important guidance is to use what strategies you feel comfortable with, provided they seem to have a positive impact on your daughter.

Other books in this series available from
Da Capo Lifelong Books by
Elizabeth Hartley-Brewer

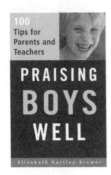

Praising Boys Well
ISBN 0-7382-1021-8
(978-0-7382-1021-6)

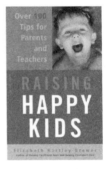

Raising Happy Kids
ISBN 0-306-81316-5

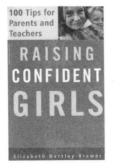

Raising a Self-Starter
ISBN 0-306-81315-7

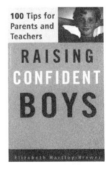

Raising Confident Boys
ISBN 1-55561-320-9

Raising Confident Girls
ISBN 1-55561-321-7

For more information, visit www.dacapopress.com.